KW-446-498

CONTENTS

TT
158.1
SEL
NF
21 APR 2004
HARTLEPOOL COPY
T46 763
528775
COU

Introduction

Self-Esteem is the sixty-sixth volume in the **Issues** series. The aim of this series is to offer up-to-date information about important issues in our world.

Self-Esteem examines self-esteem and self-confidence.

The information comes from a wide variety of sources and includes:
Government reports and statistics
Newspaper reports and features
Magazine articles and surveys
Web site material
Literature from lobby groups
and charitable organisations.

It is hoped that, as you read about the many aspects of the issues explored in this book, you will critically evaluate the information presented. It is important that you decide whether you are being presented with facts or opinions. Does the writer give a biased or an unbiased report? If an opinion is being expressed, do you agree with the writer?

Self-Esteem offers a useful starting-point for those who need convenient access to information about the many issues involved. However, it is only a starting-point. At the back of the book is a list of organisations which you may want to contact for further information.

*****

Hartlepool College of FE Infotech

T46763

285111

Self-Esteem

ISSUES

Volume 66

Editor

Craig Donnellan

Independence

Educational Publishers
Cambridge

First published by Independence
PO Box 295
Cambridge CB1 3XP
England

© Craig Donnellan 2003

Copyright
This book is sold subject to the condition that it shall not,
by way of trade or otherwise, be lent, resold, hired out or otherwise
circulated in any form of binding or cover other than that in which it
is published without the publisher's prior consent.

Photocopy licence
The material in this book is protected by copyright. However, the
purchaser is free to make multiple copies of particular articles for instructional
purposes for immediate use within the purchasing institution.
Making copies of the entire book is not permitted.

British Library Cataloguing in Publication Data
Self-Esteem – (Issues Series)
I. Donnellan, Craig II. Series
158.1

ISBN 1 86168 242 5

Printed in Great Britain
MWL Print Group Ltd

Typeset by
Claire Boyd

Cover
The illustration on the front cover is by
Pumpkin House.

The story on self-esteem

Information from KidsHealth

By D'Arcy Lyness, PhD

You can't touch it, but it affects how you feel. You can't see it, but it's there when you look at yourself in the mirror. You can't hear it, but it's there every time you talk about yourself. What is this important but mysterious thing? It's your self-esteem!

What is self-esteem?

To understand self-esteem, it helps to break the term into two words. Let's take a look at the word esteem first. Esteem is a fancy word for thinking that someone or something is important or valuing that person or thing. For example, if you really admire your friend's dad because he volunteers at the fire department, it means you hold him in high esteem. And the special trophy for the most valuable player on a team is often called an esteemed trophy. This means the trophy stands for an important accomplishment.

And self means, well, yourself! So when you put the two words together, it's easier to see what self-esteem is. It's how much you value yourself and how important you think you are. It's how you see yourself and how you feel about your achievements. Self-esteem isn't bragging about how great you are. It's more like quietly knowing that you're worth a lot (priceless, in fact!). It's not about thinking you're perfect – because nobody is – but knowing that you're worthy of being loved and accepted.

Why self-esteem is important

Self-esteem isn't like a cool pair of sneakers that you'd love to have but don't have to have. A kid needs to have self-esteem.

Good self-esteem is important because it helps you to hold your head high and feel proud of yourself and what you can do. It gives you the courage to try new things and the power to believe in yourself. It lets you respect yourself, even when you make mistakes. And when you respect yourself, adults and other kids usually respect you, too.

Having good self-esteem is also the ticket to making good choices about your mind and body. If you

If a kid moves and doesn't make friends at first in his new school, he might start to feel bad about himself if he thinks he won't ever make friends

think you're important, you'll be less likely to follow the crowd if your friends are doing something dumb or dangerous. If you have good self-esteem, you know that you're smart enough to make your own decisions. You value your safety, your feelings, your health – your whole self! Good self-esteem helps you know that every part of you is worth caring for and protecting.

How kids get self-esteem

When a baby is born, he doesn't see himself in a good way or a bad way. He doesn't think, 'I'm great!' When he lets out a big burp, or 'oh, no, this diaper makes my legs look weird!' when he sees himself in a mirror. Instead, people around the baby help him develop his self-esteem as he grows.

At first, only a baby's family might help him develop good self-esteem. They might encourage the baby when he tries to walk or praise him when he eats his cereal. They

also care for him and help him when he needs it. These positive words and actions teach him to see himself as important and feel good about himself. Even though he's so young, he's already learning that he's valuable and lovable.

As a kid gets older, many other people come into his life who can help him develop his self-esteem, such as teachers, coaches, friends, teammates, and classmates. They can help him learn things and cheer him on. They can help him figure out how to do things for himself and notice his good qualities. They can believe in him and encourage him to try again when he doesn't do something right. These types of people and activities help kids develop good self-esteem – and become kids who see themselves in a positive way and feel proud of themselves and what they are able to do.

A little on low self-esteem

Maybe you know a kid who has low self-esteem and doesn't think very highly of himself or seems to criticise himself too much. Or maybe you have low self-esteem and don't always feel very good about yourself or think you're important.

Sometimes a kid will have low self-esteem if his mother or father doesn't encourage him enough or if there is a lot of yelling at home. Other times, a kid's self-esteem can be hurt in the classroom. A teacher may make a kid feel dumb or perhaps there is a bully who says hurtful things.

For some kids, classes at school can seem so hard that they can't keep up or get the grades they'd hoped for. This can make them feel bad about themselves and hurt their self-esteem. Their self-esteem will

Feeling like you're not important can make you sad and can keep you from trying new things. It can keep you from making friends or hurt how you do at school

improve when a teacher, tutor, or counsellor can encourage them, be patient, and help them get back on track with learning. When they start to do well, their self-esteem will skyrocket!

And there are some kids who have good self-esteem, but then something happens to change that. For example, if a kid moves and doesn't make friends at first in his new school, he might start to feel bad about himself if he thinks he won't ever make friends. A kid whose parents divorce also may find that this can affect his self-esteem. He may feel bad if he begins to think he's to blame or that he's unlovable. And if a kid feels he is too fat or too thin, his self-esteem may go down if he starts thinking that means he's not good enough. Even going through the body changes of puberty – something that everybody does – can affect a kid's self-esteem.

Boosting your self-esteem

Of course it's OK to have ups and downs in your feelings, but having low self-esteem isn't OK. Feeling like you're not important can make you sad and can keep you from trying new things. It can keep you from making friends or hurt how you do at school. Having strong self-esteem is also a very big part of growing up; as you get older and face tough decisions – especially under peer pressure – the more self-esteem you have, the better. It's important to know you're worth a lot.

If you think you might have low self-esteem, try talking to an adult you trust about it. He or she may be

able to help you come up with some good ideas for building your self-esteem.

In the meantime, here are a few things that you can try to increase your self-esteem:

- Remember that your body is your own, no matter what shape, size, or colour it is. If you are worried about your weight or size, you can check with your doctor to make sure that things are OK.
- Remember that there are things about yourself you can't change – such as skin colour and shoe size – and you should accept and love these things because they are part of you.
- Remind yourself of things about your body that are cool, like, 'My legs are strong and I can skate really well.'
- When you hear negative comments in your head, mentally tell yourself to stop. The critical voice inside you will soon lose its power.
- Give yourself three compliments every day. Don't just say, 'I'm so great.' Be specific about something good about yourself, like, 'I was a good friend to Jill today' or 'I did better on that test than I thought I would.' While you're at it, before you go to bed every night, list three things in your day that really made you happy.

By focusing on the good things you do and all your great qualities, you learn to love and accept yourself, and that's the main ingredient for strong self-esteem. Even if you've got room for improvement (and who doesn't?), realising that you're valuable and important helps your self-esteem to shine.

Note: All information on KidsHealth is for educational purposes only. For specific medical advice, diagnoses, and treatment, consult your doctor.

- This information was provided by KidsHealth, one of the largest resources online for medically reviewed health information written for parent, kids, and teens. For more articles like this one, visit www.KidsHealth.org or www.TeensHealth.org

© KidsHealth.org

About self-esteem

Self-esteem: the view or picture you have of yourself as competent, worthy and lovable

Low self-esteem, misunderstood, ignored, and trivialised

Though an underlying problem of most people who seek therapy and a central issue in most relationship problems, cases of domestic violence, teen and gang violence, few therapists recognise the role of low self-esteem (LSE), or know how to treat it. Consequently, people go from therapist to therapist, who label their problems as depression, anger, anxiety, etc. when these are merely symptoms of LSE. Off target, these interventions provide some immediate relief but do not produce lasting results. Low self-esteem is the underlying cause of most cases involving:

- Fear
- Anxiety
- Anger
- Panic attacks (self-esteem attacks)
- Dependence and lack of assertiveness
- Depression
- Eating disorders
- Domestic violence
- Teen and gang violence
- Addictive behaviours
- Relationship problems
- Child-abuse
- Social anxiety disorder and other anxiety problems
- Avoidant personality disorders
- Dependent personality disorders

Yet, most therapists treat the symptoms and not the core issue.

They do not understand how low self-esteem works to interfere with and destroy lives; therefore few therapists specialise in self-esteem issues.

The impact of low self-esteem

Once low self-esteem is formed, the fear and anxiety that accompanies it affects everything a person does, says, and thinks.

Many who have LSE avoid seeking new jobs, initiating relationships, or learning new skills for fear of rejection or failure. Many avoid social settings and refrain from sharing their opinions for the same reasons. Some isolate, become people pleasers, and remain passive. Others get aggressive and cause havoc in their relationships. All people with LSE sabotage their lives to some degree.

Some become underachievers, achieving far less than they are capable of because they are paralysed by fear. Others, driven to prove to themselves and others that they are adequate and deserving, become overachievers, probably becoming more successful than they would have if they didn't have low self-esteem. These overachievers often become workaholics, sometimes to the detriment of their families, creating relationship problems.

You cannot necessarily tell that a person has low self-esteem because many who have LSE become experts at hiding their feelings and maintaining the appearance of control, even though this is not what they feel on the inside. In fact, many very successful people in high level careers actually suffer from low self-esteem, though only those close to them are aware they have LSE.

People go from therapist to therapist, who label their problems as depression, anger, anxiety, etc. when these are merely symptoms of low self-esteem

When people with LSE do something they perceive as stupid or inappropriate, they instantly feel humiliated and suffer from 'self-esteem attacks'. At these moments they desperately want to run and hide, though this is often not possible. They may plummet into depression and devastation, episodes that may last minutes, hours, days, or even weeks. Afterwards they feel even more embarrassed to face the people who they think are aware of their problem.

Anger problems, domestic and teen violence have at their core low self-esteem. The most effective and lasting treatment is that of a combination of working to improve one's self-esteem along with learning techniques to manage anger. All too often, however, when people seek therapy or enter into anger management classes, self-esteem is not even discussed.

- If you have seen one or more therapists and are still suffering from one of these problems, you must read *Breaking the Chain of Low Self-Esteem!* Scores of readers have identified LSE as their real issue after reading this book.

- The above information is from the Self-Esteem Institute's web site which can be found at www.TheSelfEsteeminstitute.com

© 2002 The Self-Esteem Institute

Does 'self-esteem' really exist?

By Mark Tyrrell

Low self-esteem, a cause and symptom of depression, anxiety and anger problems, has become the modern pariah.

Low self-esteem, a rope that binds; preventing us pursuing our dreams and enjoying simple things that 'other people enjoy'. We talk of 'self-esteem issues' and nod sagely to one another.

We use the words but do we examine what they really mean? You can't hold self-esteem in your hand or take the kids to see it on a Sunday afternoon. So, what actually is self-esteem?

Self-esteem: a definition

Many religions' scriptures teach that pride and arrogance are terrible sins, the idea being that you can't worship yourself and a god at the same time. Supposedly, if you are 'full of yourself', you have little space for anything or anyone else.

However, real self-esteem is not arrogance or self-love or vanity. Real self-esteem consists of:

- An appreciation of what we can do.
- An honest respect for our own abilities, potentials and value.

- Knowing our strengths and trusting in them.
- An appreciation and open acceptance of our limitations.
- An acceptance of these limitations whilst understanding that some limitations can be overcome.
- A freedom from over-concern with what we imagine others think of us whilst accepting these perceptions do play a part in everyday life but do not determine who we are.
- Having a strong sense of who we are.

The self-esteem movement and self-affirmations

I'm sure you've seen and possibly read some of the countless self-help books out there. Some of these encourage us to 'love ourselves' or repeat 'positive affirmations' to ourselves everyday in order to 're-programme' ourselves.

Does this work? And if it does work what does it say about human beings?

Belief in yourself is important, but so are the skills that stop you having to work so hard at believing!

If I am a bullying, vindictive sadist would it be wrong for me to experience self-reproach or even self-disgust or should I just tell myself one hundred times a day I am a good human being whilst continuing in the same way?

Balance in all things

Feeling bad about aspects of our behaviour, be it selfishness, laziness, intolerance or aggressiveness is valid feedback. We *can* judge ourselves and feel bad about ourselves sometimes.

If I have behaved terribly then I need to feel badly about that particular time for a while but *not* badly about my whole identity. To state 'I am worthless to the core' on the basis of one mistake is unrealistic. Because, equally, I can find times when I have behaved decently or done well.

The essential difference

There is a difference between telling myself: 'I am a totally worthless human being, because last week I was rude to the in-laws, and I will always be hopeless and hopeless in every area.' (low-self-esteem) and 'I behaved really badly last night with those specific people at that specific time'.

This accepts responsibility but doesn't damn one's whole personality and life as worthless (good self-esteem).

So we can still be self-critical and have good self-esteem at the same time. And we do this by not generalising about our mistakes and weaknesses to include everything about ourselves.

To sum up: Belief in yourself is important, but so are the skills that stop you having to work so hard at believing!

The importance of developing skills as a foundation for good self-esteem

So, now we come to the crux of the matter. If I tell myself that 'every day I am becoming more and more confident in social situations' then I go out and feel terribly shy and embarrassed, what do you think it is sensible for me to believe?

Should I believe what I have been endlessly repeating to myself, or should I believe my actual everyday experience?

If, however, someone were to come along (and I hope they do) and teach me conversational skills, relaxation techniques and thinking skills then I can start to experience feeling more comfortable socially. This lets me know that I am better socially and when I know I don't need merely to believe.

'Soft skills' for low self-esteem

Learning sports, languages, practical skills like driving or carpentry can all raise a sense of competency. However, handling our emotions effectively is also a skill. Emotional skills are sometimes termed as 'soft skills'. Some of these soft skills include:

- Being able to 'read' the emotions of others.
- Knowing when others are angry, upset, unsettled etc.
- Being sensitive to others whilst realising that we, too, have a position within any given situation.
- Having empathy. Being able to 'put ourselves in the position of the other person'.
- Being able to assert our point of view. When appropriate 'speaking up for ourselves' assertively.
- Having an effective communication style.
- Being able to make ourselves understood and being able to compromise to the benefit of all involved.
- Having good rapport skills and being able to forge and maintain friendships.

- Observing our own emotional ebbs and flows.
- Knowing how to manage our own anger and 'low times' so we are not swamped by our own emotions.
- Understanding our own needs for company, rest, creative stimulation, healthy lifestyle, achievable goals, attention and intimacy so that we can feel a sense of control.
- Making allowances for these needs in our everyday life.
- Having wide interests and activities (as far as possible). So we are not just 'Mother', 'Wife', 'Co-worker', 'Father' etc.
- Being able to manage stress in our lives – which relates to some of the above skills.
- Understanding the paramount importance of the company we keep. Do we just mix with people who bring us down or do we associate with others who are positive and fun?

A person's self-esteem seems to match the extent to which they have the above skills in place.

These skills are what we focus on in our Free Self-Confidence and Self-Esteem Course and on our Self-Confidence Trainer CD.

The perfect self-esteem trap

'Heaven would be just a little better if there weren't quite so many angels playing harps.'

Of course some people do have a wide variety of skills and talents and still seem to suffer from low self-esteem! You may be a perfectionist or know somebody who is. You know the idea, 'Nothing is ever good enough.'

Demanding the impossible from yourself and then falling short is

---

Some people do have a wide variety of skills and talents and still seem to suffer from low self-esteem! You may be a perfectionist or know somebody who is. You know the idea, 'Nothing is ever good enough'

obviously a trap! Knowing when we have done a 'pretty damn good job' and giving ourselves an appropriate level of credit is actually an important 'soft skill' (as is taking appropriate responsibility for our screw-ups).

So, if someone wants to have perfect 'soft skills' then they need to stop talking to themselves in ways which they wouldn't even consider talking to other people.

I remember being stunned when a school friend confided to me how disappointed he was for only getting 96% in a French test. He said he 'should' have got 100%. Our teacher was pleased with him, his parents were pleased with him but, for him, the losing of that 4% made the whole exam a failure. I won't tell you what I 'achieved' in the same test but I can tell you I was pleased to have understood any of it.

It's great to have high aims and expectations for ourselves but we need to temper this with an appreciation that we are human.

Self-esteem – a summary

So, rather than trying to convince ourselves desperately that we are worthy of great self-admiration through a series of unsubtle brainwashing, the way towards good self-esteem seems to be through the development of skills, specifically the so-called 'soft skills'.

When we are less self-conscious, less negatively biased and more open to our own abilities to adapt, progress and develop then we can have the spare capacity to forget about self-esteem and begin to enjoy and participate more fully in life.

- The above information is from Uncommon Knowledge's web site: www.uncommon-knowledge.co.uk

© Uncommon Knowledge

The costs and causes of low self-esteem

Information from the Joseph Rowntree Foundation (JRF)

There is a widespread view that low self-esteem is a risk factor for a broad range of psychological and behavioural problems. However, neither public discussion nor decisions to invest in prevention and treatment have been strongly informed or guided by hard evidence, either about the effects or the causes of low self-esteem. A review of the available research evidence, by Nicholas Emler (London School of Economics), aimed to fill this gap. The review found that:

- There is not perfect agreement among researchers about the nature of self-esteem. The most significant division is between the view that self-esteem is a generalised feeling about the self, and the view that it is the sum of a set of judgements about one's value, worthiness, and competence in various domains.
- Despite imperfect agreement about its nature, levels of self-esteem can be reliably and easily measured.
- The design of much, perhaps most, published research means it cannot show whether self-esteem has a causal influence on behaviour patterns. The most informative evidence comes from longitudinal studies, following the same individuals over time. This shows that:

– relatively low self-esteem is not a risk factor for delinquency, violence towards others (including child and partner abuse), drug use, alcohol abuse, educational under-attainment or racism;

– relatively low self-esteem is a risk factor for suicide, suicide attempts and depression, for teenage pregnancy, and for victimisation by others. In each case, however, this risk factor is one of several and probably interacts with others;

– there are indications that childhood self-esteem is associated with adolescent eating disorders and with economic outcomes – earnings, continuity of employment – in early adulthood, but the causal mechanisms involved remain unclear.

- Low self-esteem in an absolute sense is rare. Most of the comparative research contrasts the consequences of very high self-esteem with more moderate levels.
- The strongest influences upon self-esteem are the individual's parents. Parenting style, physical and particularly sexual abuse play a significant role, as do genetic factors.
- Planned interventions can raise self-esteem but knowledge of why particular interventions work, or whether their effects are more than short term, is very limited.

■ The full report, *Self-esteem: The costs and causes of low self-worth*, by Nicholas Emler, is published for the Foundation by YPS (ISBN 1 84263 020 2, price £15.95).

■ The above information is from the Joseph Rowntree Foundation's (JRF) web site which can be found at www.jrf.org.uk

© Joseph Rowntree Foundation (JRF)

Answering misconceptions about self-esteem

1. Does self-esteem mean feeling good about yourself?

Self-esteem is an experience. It is a particular way of experiencing the self. It is a good deal more than a mere feeling. It involves emotional, evaluative, and cognitive components. It also entails certain action dispositions: to move toward life rather than away from it; to move toward consciousness rather than away from it; to treat facts with respect rather than denial; to operate self-responsibly rather than the opposite.

Self-esteem is the disposition to experience oneself as being competent to cope with the basic challenges of life and of being worthy of happiness. It is confidence in the efficacy of our mind, in our ability to think. By extension, it is confidence in our ability to learn, to make appropriate choices and decisions, and respond effectively to change. It is also the experience that success, achievement, fulfilment – happiness – are right and natural for us.

Self-esteem is not the euphoria of buoyancy that may be temporarily induced by a drug, a compliment, or a love affair. It is not an illusion or hallucination. Lots of things (some of them quite dubious) can make us 'feel good' – for a while. If self-esteem is not grounded in reality if it

By Dr Nathaniel Branden

is not built over time through the appropriate operation of mind, for example, through operating consciously, self-responsibly, and with integrity – it is not self-esteem.

2. Doesn't a teacher's pre-occupation with nurturing a student's self-esteem get in the way of academic achievement?

That depends on the teacher's understanding of self-esteem and what is required to nurture it. If a teacher treats students with respect, avoids ridicule and other belittling remarks, deals with everyone fairly and justly, and projects a strong, benevolent conviction about every student's potential, then that teacher is supporting both self-esteem and the process of learning and mastering the challenges. For such a teacher, self-esteem is tied to reality, not to faking reality.

In contrast, however, if a teacher tries to nurture self-esteem by empty praise that bears no relationship to the students' actual accomplishments, dropping all objective standards – allowing young people to believe that the only passport to self-esteem they

need is the recognition that they are 'unique' – then self-esteem is undermined and so is academic achievement.

We help people to grow by holding rational expectations up to them, not by expecting nothing of them; the latter is a message of contempt. Research indicates that there is a significant relationship between self-esteem and academic achievement, and that if we can raise a student's self-esteem, academic improvement tends to follow.

3. Can anyone develop high self-esteem or is it the prerogative of a fortunate minority?

People of average intelligence or better can, in principle, grow into psychologically healthy adults. Obviously parents, teachers, and other adults can do a great deal to make the road to self-esteem easier or harder. Sometimes, where there are deep psychic wounds and traumas left unresolved since childhood, a decent level of self-esteem can be very difficult to achieve. In such cases, psychotherapy may be necessary.

But I have never met anyone utterly devoid of self-esteem and I have never met anyone unable to grow in self-esteem, assuming appropriate opportunities for learning exist in their worldspace.

4. Doesn't a focus on self-esteem encourage excessive and inappropriate self-absorption?

Rationally, one does not focus on self-esteem per se; one focuses on the practices that support and nurture self-esteem such as the practice of living consciously, of self-acceptance, of self-responsibility, of self-assertiveness of purposefulness, and of integrity, as I discuss in the Six Pillars of Self-Esteem.

Self-esteem demands a high reality-orientation; it is grounded in a reverent respect for facts and truth.

Excessive and inappropriate self-absorption is symptomatic of poor self-esteem, not high self-esteem. If there is something we are confident about, we do not obsess about it – we get on with living.

5. Can't one have too much self-esteem?

No, not if one is talking about reality-based self-esteem rather than grandiosity. It is no more possible to have too much self-esteem than it is to have too much physical or mental health. But sometimes when people lack adequate self-esteem they fall into arrogance, boasting, and grandiosity as a defense mechanism – a compensatory strategy. Their problem is not that they have too big an ego but they have too small a one.

Further, let me say that high self-esteem is not egotism, as some people mistakenly imagine. Egotism is an attitude of bragging, boasting, arrogating to oneself qualities one does not possess, throwing one's weight around, seeking to prove one's superiority to others – all evidences of insecurity and underdeveloped self-esteem.

6. Isn't self-esteem essentially a godless pursuit?

Is watching one's diet and eating intelligently a 'godless pursuit'? Is exercising? Is striving to learn and grow? Is the pursuit of self-development and self-realisation 'godless'? Why would one think in such terms?

With regard to self-esteem, I do not see 'God' as relevant, one way or the other, unless you believe in a malevolent God who wishes human beings to face the challenges of life in a state of terror and paralysis.

The plain truth is, some people with good self-esteem believe in God and others with good self-esteem do not.

7. Isn't self-esteem determined by parental upbringing?

How some parents wish it were! But the truth is, many factors influence our self-esteem. Certainly parental upbringing is important; parents can make the road to self-esteem easier or harder – but they cannot determine the ultimate level of their child's self-esteem. Neither can teachers or other adults. Neither can biology – nor birth experiences. Yet all these factors can play a role. And among these factors, none is likely to be as important as the influence of parents, primarily through the values they instil, which can lead a child toward or away from growing self-esteem.

However, we must remember the role that each individual plays, through the choices and decisions we make every day.

We are not merely clay on which external forces write. We are active contestants in the drama. As adults we carry primary responsibility for the level of self-esteem we develop.

8. Isn't self-esteem the consequence of approval from 'significant others'?

No. If we live semi-consciously, non-responsibly, and without integrity, it will not matter who loves us – we will not love ourselves. When people betray their mind and judgement ('sell their souls') to win the approval of their 'significant others', they may win that approval, but their self-esteem suffers.

What shall it profit us to win the approval of the whole world and lose our own?

It is commonly held that among young people the approval of 'significant others' does profoundly affect self-esteem, and to some extent this is doubtless true – but one has to wonder about the reality of a self-esteem that is so precarious that it crashes easily if that approval is withdrawn.

9. Doesn't the possession of good looks, popularity, and wealth almost guarantee self-esteem?

People who lack self-esteem sometimes think so, but the truth is that in today's world there are celebrities who have physical beauty, millions of adoring fans, and millions of dollars – and still they cannot get through a day without drugs. They live with severe anxiety or depression or both. Good looks, popularity, and wealth guarantee nothing – if one does not have the self-esteem to support them.

Lacking such self-esteem, it is very easy to feel like an impostor, waiting to be 'found out – and waiting for all one's advantages to be blown away.

Even among young people where the assets mentioned above tend to be more important, the relation of these assets to self-esteem is fragile at best; long-term, they are far from an adequate foundation for the experience of competence and worth.

10. Does praising appropriate behaviour nurture self-esteem?

That depends on what is meant by 'praising'. If we see a child acting consciously and responsibly, and we acknowledge this behaviour with recognition and appreciation, we may increase the likelihood that such behaviour will be repeated. If we ridicule, punish, or ignore it, we may produce the opposite result. Either way, we may indirectly influence the child's self-esteem (although not necessarily).

But to be effective, 'praise – or more exactly, recognition – should be reality-based, calibrated to the significance of the child's actions (in other words, not extravagant or grandiose), and directed at the child's behaviour rather than his or her character. Sweeping statements such as 'You're a perfect angel,' or 'You're always such a good girl,' or 'You're always so kind and loving,' are not helpful; rather than nurture self-esteem, they tend to evoke anxiety, since the child knows there are times when they are not true.

Even with these restrictions, praise or recognition needs to be administered cautiously, so as to avoid turning a child into an approval-addict. We want a child to experience the intrinsic pleasure that flows from appropriate behaviour.

Parents can make the road to self-esteem easier or harder – but they cannot determine the ultimate level of their child's self-esteem

We want the child to become the source of his or her own approval, not always waiting eagerly for ours. So we need to avoid bombarding a child with our 'evaluations'.

11. Isn't it true that if you have high self-esteem, nothing bothers you?

Some enthusiasts for self-esteem believe good self-esteem solves nearly all the important problems of life. This is untrue.

Struggle is intrinsic to life. Sooner or later everyone experiences anxiety and pain – and while self-esteem can make one less susceptible, it cannot make one impervious. To offer a simple example: If someone you love dies, does having good self-esteem mean the loss won't bother you? Clearly not.

Think of self-esteem as the immune system of consciousness. If you have a healthy immune system, you might become ill, but you are less likely to; if you do become ill, you will likely recover faster – your resilience is greater. Similarly, if you have high self-esteem, you might still know times of emotional suffering, but less often and with a faster recovery – your resilience is greater.

A well-developed sense of self is a necessary but not a sufficient condition of your well-being. Its presence does not guarantee fulfilment, but its absence guarantees some measure of anxiety, frustration and despair.

Some people, when they face new challenges initially perceived as intimidating or overwhelming, may suffer a temporary dip in the level of their self-esteem. Then, as they persevere and master the new challenges, self-esteem rises again. Such fluctuations are normal.

© 2003 National Association for Self-Esteem (NASE)

Self-esteem diamond explanation

1 Personality comes from the decisions we have made about who we are. If we have decided that we are a kind, loving, truthful, responsible human being, and we practise performing in the ways that display those traits then we are living professionally and in integrity.

2 Performance comes from the way we do our job. If we are skilled and do our work reliably and impeccably, we have either chosen a profession in which we have natural talent or we have learned the skills necessary to do the job professionally.

3 Presentation comes from the way we respect and care for our body, space and things. If we have decided to present our space, our things and ourselves as clean, healthy, well kept and appreciated we are displaying our decision to be a professional, respectful of ourselves and others.

4 Self-Esteem is an ongoing process that comes from connecting with our soul and spiritual potential through self-acceptance, meditation, prayer, release, communing with nature and/or requesting strength from our higher power, source, spirit or god. It is a process of balancing our lives by consciously attending to our Soul – personality; Mind – performance and our Body – presentation.

5 Professionalism, high self-esteem and integrity come from being whole and in balance, from 'the experience of being capable of meeting life's challenges and being worthy of happiness'. Our decision to be a reliable performer, and respectful in our presentation guarantees our capability. Our decision to stay connected with our unlimited potential assures us that we are worthy of happiness and brings us into harmony and peace.

■ The above information is from La Belle Foundation's Self-Esteem web site which can be found at www.selfesteem.org

© La Belle Foundation

Professional self-esteem diamond

Self-esteem and eating disorders

Information from the Eating Disorders Association (EDA)

Self-esteem

What is it and why does it matter?

'Self-esteem is a person's unconditional appreciation of her/himself. It matters because people who do not value themselves feel unworthy. They can then treat themselves and others badly, usually unintentionally. Low self-esteem is often a major factor in abuse, depression, crime, loneliness, low achievement, addiction, mental illness and unhappiness.'

The above definition is taken from *The Self-Esteem Directory*.

The unconditional aspect of self-esteem is of fundamental importance. If we accept ourselves without 'conditions' we can accept praise or criticism without it adversely affecting out sense of self-worth. It also means we have realistic expectations of ourselves with a clear view of our strengths and weaknesses. We are no longer dependent on other people's view of ourselves. This is why self-esteem is so important for learning. If we can trust ourselves, we can take the risk of making a mistake.

Unconditional appreciation of ourselves means accepting ourselves as we are, including our body, our feelings and our abilities. It means going beyond 'image' and recognising our fundamental worth as a human being. In other words, recognising our ability to love, experience joy, communicate and be creative as well as acknowledging that we can be lazy, destructive or cruel. By appreciating both our negative and positive aspects, we take responsibility for ourselves and grow.

The link between self-esteem and mental health has been increasingly studied in recent years. Dr Alex Yellowlees, a Consultant Psychiatrist in Scotland, produced the workbook, *Working with Eating Disorders and Self-Esteem*. Dr Yellowlees and his team did extensive research on this and developed the detailed workbook based on the importance of positive self-esteem. If self-esteem is critically low, it can lead to dissatisfaction with ourselves and may develop into such problems as eating disorders. Dr Yellowlees suggests dividing self-esteem into two key elements: self-competence and self-worth.

Self-competence and self-worth

Self-competence is to do with having a sense of self-confidence, that one is up to the task of living. It involves:

- being able to cope with the basic challenges of life
- having confidence in our ability to think for ourselves
- having confidence in our right to attempt to meet our needs, physical and emotional.
- having the confidence to assert our rights and achieve our goals.

Self-worth is more to do with our sense of self-respect and the value we place on ourselves. It involves a sense of:

- value
- significance
- empowerment or being able to do what we want to do
- basic goodness or virtue
- adequacy
- being entitled to personal happiness and the enjoyment of the rewards of our efforts.

Low self-esteem – these are some of the feelings and attitudes involved:

- dependency, feeling helpless and needing approval, hostility towards others
- depressions anxiety, preferring to give in
- poor general health
- feelings of apathy, of being powerless, isolation, not worth loving, withdrawal, too keen to please and follow others.
- tendency to criticise and be negative about other people
- if you feel negative about yourself, you tend to think everyone else does too.

Low self-esteem and its relationship with eating disorders

Self-esteem cannot be permanently raised by dieting or weight loss – it is simply tackling the problem at the wrong level, on the outside, rather than the inside of the person and how s/he really feels about themselves.

Some of the thinking and behaviour associated with eating disorders can be seen as attempts to raise very low self-esteem.

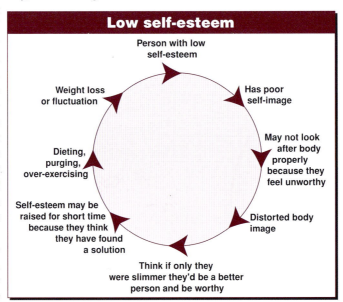

Low self-esteem

- Person with low self-esteem
- Has poor self-image
- May not look after body properly because they feel unworthy
- Distorted body image
- Think if only they were slimmer they'd be a better person and be worthy
- Self-esteem may be raised for short time because they think they have found a solution
- Dieting, purging, over-exercising
- Weight loss or fluctuation

Celebrating our achievements does not come easily, there are often cultural taboos to overcome especially for girls. However, in other cultures celebrating achievement is seen as perfectly acceptable. For example, Masai communities in East Africa compose and sing 'Boasting' songs as a means of uniting and lifting the community spirit. Receiving and accepting compliments, which is beneficial to the development of a healthy self-esteem, is 'not the done thing' in our society!!

We downgrade our self-esteem by giving credit to others not ourselves

---

We downgrade our self-esteem by:
- emphasising what we did not achieve rather than what we did
- trivialising our skills, knowledge or gifts
- giving credit to others not ourselves
- spending more time talking about our mistakes, rather than our successes/achievements
- giving more importance to other's criticisms than compliments
- putting ourselves down.

Re-energising self-esteem
- Try to remember you are worthy
- Talk to others, tell the people you trust about the things you find difficult
- Identify what you're good at and give yourself praise for it
- Try to remember other people have needs too
- Life is just wonderful! We all have our dreams and the right to dream them
- Self-esteem is the most precious gift you have – treasure it and yourself.

Taken from the 'Girlpower' pack

■ The above information is from the Eating Disorders Association (EDA). See page 41 for their address details.
© Eating Disorders Association (EDA)

Body image and appearance

On the face of it, girls seem to be confident about their bodies and their appearance. It seems that they know that they 'should' say that weight isn't important and that they are comfortable with how they look. But, beneath the surface, girls are under great pressure from many directions to be pretty and thin, and this is reflected in how they view themselves and how they behave.

The 'girl power' viewpoint is reflected in the 78% of girls who say they are happy with their body and the 79% who say they are happy with the way they look.

But most girls agree that they do worry about how they look.
■ And 42% believe their life would be easier if they were more attractive. This concern about their appearance and their weight reflects the girls' strong desire to fit in with their peer group and be seen as attractive and popular.
■ 'Attractiveness' is often linked to achieving a certain 'look'
■ Generally that which matches the thin and pretty images seen in the media
■ Often combined with an underlying view that people who have the right 'look' are more successful – particularly models, pop stars and actors.

The pressure to conform to a certain look comes from several directions
■ From worrying about what their friends and other girls will think of them
■ Because of worry about what boys will think
■ And because of the images they see in the media (88% feel that there is a lot of pressure from the media to 'look' perfect).

The most compelling evidence that girls are not happy with their bodies, despite what they say, is that 19% are on a diet
■ With fairly high numbers dieting even among 11- and 12-year-olds.

■ The above information is from *Today's Girl – Tomorrow's Woman*, a special report from the Guide Association. See their web site at www.girlguiding.org.uk

© The Guide Association

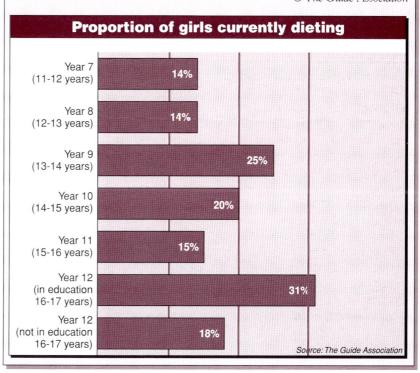

Proportion of girls currently dieting

Year 7 (11-12 years)	14%
Year 8 (12-13 years)	14%
Year 9 (13-14 years)	25%
Year 10 (14-15 years)	20%
Year 11 (15-16 years)	15%
Year 12 (in education 16-17 years)	31%
Year 12 (not in education 16-17 years)	18%

Source: The Guide Association

A valuable trait

High self-esteem has manifold benefits in terms of mental and physical wellbeing and it's never too late to build it up – at home, work or school. Brigid McConville reports

It can be tempting to dismiss 'self-esteem' as one of those faddish buzzwords used to sell Californian-style self-help books. But there is no doubt that it has a serious and well-researched impact on health and wellbeing across all age groups and settings – in schools, at home and in the workplace. Alex Yellowlees, a consultant psychiatrist at Murray Royal Hospital in Perth, Scotland, is a specialist in eating disorders and a believer in the importance of self-esteem for mental wellbeing. He says there are two fundamental pillars of self-esteem. The first is self-worth, 'that deep-seated sense that one is of genuine value'. The second is self-competence, 'the feeling that "I can cope" – that one is up to the challenges of everyday life'.

People with a strong sense of both have high levels of self-esteem, which keeps them mentally healthy and able to cope. Those with a weak sense of both, he says, can be vulnerable to depression, anxiety, bulimia, anorexia and dysfunctional relationships. Those who have a strong sense of self-worth – but little belief in their own abilities – 'are popularly regarded as big-headed egotists who are full of themselves'. In fact, their problem may well be defensiveness due to low self-esteem.

Their opposites – people with a strong sense of their own abilities but a low sense of self-worth – tend to be overachievers. They are often charismatic celebrity figures, says Yellowlees, but can be prone to addictions and eating disorders. 'Other people say "Wow, you're fantastic". But inside they feel terrible. These are also the workaholics who need ever more achievements to prop up their sense of self. They write a book, it gives them a boost, but when that wears off they have to write another. They can also be highly dangerous – the dictators of the world.'

So far so good, but if you've been brought up by over-critical parents, educated in the school of 'hard knocks' or employed by an authoritarian, perfectionist boss (another face of low self-esteem), how can you ever recover?

> ## People with a strong sense of self-worth and self-confidence have high levels of self-esteem, which keeps them mentally healthy and able to cope

---

Clearly, someone who has had traumatic life experiences, such as physical or sexual abuse, will need psychotherapy or psychiatric help. Equally, 'it's not enough to do positive affirmations in front of your mirror'. Rather, Yellowlees points to 'a small number of very well researched, pragmatic strategies' that can build self-esteem – and believes most people can use these strategies to improve their lives.

As he points out, adults are capable of learning new skills to fill the gaps in their competence. Someone who is a brilliant administrator but painfully shy, for example, could polish up their social skills. While someone who is great at communicating, but has a chaotic office, could do a computer course.

Building up the other pillar of self-esteem (self-worth) involves pursuing self-awareness.

'This could mean going to a counsellor with experience in this field and discussing your relationship with a remote father. It could mean talking to friends and realising it wasn't that way for everybody.' Self-help groups, women's or men's groups, assertive training, workshops on self-esteem, building a network of positive friends – all these will help build self-worth, he says. Alternatively, it could mean finding a way to be a good parent to yourself – as the self-esteem 'lobby' puts it, 'it's never too late to have a happy childhood'. Indeed, the best way to build high self-esteem is to have parents who feel good about themselves and confident about their own abilities. So while adults may have to work on themselves, 'we can make things a hundred per cent better for our children'.

He cites two types of dysfunctional family: the rigid, authoritarian type and the permissive type with no boundaries. Both are just as bad as each other when it comes to building children's self-esteem, says Yellowlees. He advises: 'Accept children for who they are and respect their individuality. Set realistic but flexible limits to their behaviour – and have realistic expectations of them. Do not make your love for them conditional on their achievements or appearance.'

Ruth Nash knows the power of self-esteem – from both a personal and a professional perspective. 'I had a problem with self-esteem during my teens,' she explains. 'I suffered from severe depression and eating disorders. I didn't like myself or my body. I had such a low sense of self-worth that it played havoc with my life. I was treated with anti-depressants for years.'

Joining a confidence-building group helped. 'I learned not to be so critical of myself and stopped trying to be perfect. I feel very strongly that there is too much pressure on girls and boys to look good. You have to be slim and blonde to be "attractive" and accepted. The group taught me to think positively. I learned that – like other people with low self-esteem – I was saying "yes" to things I didn't want to do. It was also a help to talk with other people in the same boat.'

Although it was a struggle, by the age of 20 (she is now 22) Nash had regained her confidence. 'It's been a slog, but I've got it together now. I have a responsible job as a play work manager, liaising with parents and social services. But I know how to handle it – and how to ask for help if I need it.'

Nash is using her past experience – and knowledge from a course on the subject – to help boost young people's self-esteem at the Fun Club,

---

'Teenagers can send us up the wall by being bloody minded. But they have a need to do things differently'

an afterschool club for 4- to 14-year-olds in Inkberrow, Worcestershire. There's been a noticeable difference in the behaviour of one particularly difficult child, as she explains: 'He was very aggressive and disruptive. He'd use bad language and laugh if you challenged him. He was very demanding – and he couldn't handle praise.'

Initially, Nash learned to identify how he was feeling by his attitude and body language. 'That meant I could intervene and distract him.' (Although sometimes, when he was winding her up, she admits, 'I just had to walk away.') 'Instead of saying "no" all the time, I praised him for any good behaviour. I also asked him to help with tasks and gave him responsibilities – like keeping an eye on the younger children.' Nash also liaised closely with his parents – who took the same approach at home. Their persistence paid off. Now, a year and a half later, he is a different child. 'When we tell him he's been really great he says "thanks", instead of "no I'm not". He's more popular with the other children – he can play cooperatively. He's told me he really likes coming to the club.'

Sheila Munro, who lives in London, also came to recognise self-esteem as an issue via a personal route – and has since become professionally involved in the area.

'I was at my wits' end as a parent. My son was aged nine and I found it a very difficult stage. We weren't getting on and so I did a parenting course with Parentline Plus. It made communication between us much easier and I felt much more confident in what I was doing as a parent.' Today Munro works as a consultant and trainer for the organisation.

'Parents come on our courses saying they find their child difficult. They are unhappy and desperately want to do their best for their children. Then they start to talk about themselves – and it becomes apparent that parents who outwardly seem confident and able, don't feel good about themselves.' Issues of guilt and anxiety about not being a good parent come to the fore. 'They don't come on the course "to do self-esteem", but that's what emerges. We respond by doing exercises which help parents to look at what they do well – and to appreciate themselves and each other,' she says. 'The more you appreciate yourself, the more you are able to convey appreciation of your children.' Munro also works on practical parenting skills to build self-esteem in children. 'We talk about how to avoid labels in the family – being "the clever one" can be just as oppressive as being "the stupid one". We talk about the importance of really listening to your children – which plays a key role in helping them to feel valued. The beauty of it is that the more children have self-regard and feel good about themselves, the more likely they are to be healthy, happy children who, as a by-product, behave in cooperative, social ways.'

Parents, too, are better placed to deal with problems and encourage self-esteem if they understand their children's developmental needs, says Munro, citing teenagers as an example. 'Teenagers can send us up the wall by being bloody minded. But they have a need to do things differently, to stretch their mental powers by arguing. They also need to withdraw, be private, sulk and be broody because they are developing their own emotional life. It might be hard to live with, but it helps parents to understand that this is a part of healthy development.'

Munro is author of *Parenting Matters*, a publication that is widely used on Parentline Plus courses – one of which was attended by Millie, a single parent with a teenager and, again, someone who was struggling with low self-esteem.

Prior to joining the course, Millie described her family life as 'world war three on a daily basis', as she struggled with guilt about her divorce. 'The course made me realise I wasn't listening enough to my daughter. There was an instant change in our relationship. It has stopped us rowing all the time and has helped me to look after myself. One of the most important things I got out of it was reassurance that I was all right as a mother.'

Away from the domestic sphere, self-esteem has also emerged as a crucial workplace issue, according to Jeremy Glyn, project director for the Pacific Institute, an international organisation specialising in the development of organisations and neighbourhood renewal. (The Institute uses its work with businesses in over 40 countries worldwide to subsidise its other activities with people who are unemployed and in prison – and with over a third of local education authorities in the UK.)

'A lot of our work is in helping management with the development of leaders, with corporate culture change and optimum performance,' says Glyn. He argues that the commitment of individuals to their

work, along with their confidence and self-motivation, are crucial to performance. But not only are senior managers ill-equipped to deal with such personal and psychological issues, they themselves can also feel isolated and unsupported. 'Very seldom does anyone congratulate them. They only get the knocks and criticism – and they can't talk openly with their colleagues,' he says.

Glyn uses psychological techniques to build self-esteem in the workplace, starting at board level. In a recent survey of the organisation's work with managing directors, every respondent gave a 'five out of five' rating for the gains they had made in self-esteem. So what does it mean for their organisations? He cites one company that seemed to have a belief that it would never meet its financial targets. After working with them, he says, 'they met their targets for the first time in 15 years'.

But isn't this just brainwashing, using Japanese-style tactics to make more profits out of the workforce? If so, argues Glyn, it is a matter of individual choice, 'and we've all got

garbage to get rid of'. It's a philosophy that fits with Yellowlees' assertion that 'boosting self-esteem not only leads to better job satisfaction, but to better mental and physical health too – because we take care of our bodies more, eat well and have fun'. No wonder self-esteem has become a buzzword of the new millennium.

■ The above information is an article from *Health Development Today*, the magazine produced by the Health Development Agency. For more details visit their web site at www.hda-online.org.uk

© *Health Development Agency*

False self-esteem

(Bullying, controlling, neurotic and victim behaviour)

Neurotic pride encourages isolation and depression

Healthy high self-esteem is characterised by an open mind and flexible, warm, friendly, outgoing personality with a high standard of personal conduct. There is self-respect and self-love, combined with respect for others ('You're OK, I'm OK').

High self-esteem people can afford to be kind and generous because they are not easily exploited, bullied or manipulated.

You may not always like what they say but you know where you stand with them and you can trust their honesty and integrity.

Low self-esteem is characterised by more closed, rigid and defensive (territorial hostility) behaviours and opinions. The world is repeatedly experienced as threatening, demanding or unsupportive, which leads to free-flowing anxiety or constant frustration and anger.

If the anger is internalised the experience of depression is created.

Ingrained feelings of inadequacy and a deep inner fear of inferiority is defended (hidden, compensated

for) by false self-esteem (also known as neurotic pride) which is a sense of personal value and safety based on accumulation of achievements, power or status, combined with denigration of other people, aggressive emotions, control, bullying, fear, manipulation or exploitation of others.

The subconscious agenda and perception underlying false self-esteem are:

'Neither of us is OK, but I'm going to make you think I am!'

Maintaining neurotic pride takes up lots of our time and energy. Letting go of these behaviours and healing the underlying wounds, negative self-beliefs and judgements puts us in touch with:
■ solid personal value, experiencing mutual love and respect in relationships
■ freedom and aliveness not based on the constantly vulnerable pedestal of being in control or being superior.

■ The above information is an extract from Sunflower Health's web site: www.stress-counselling.co.uk

© *2002 Michael J. Meredith*

Happiness is all in the mind

Optimists are healthier and enjoy themselves more. Is it possible always to look on the brighter side of life?

As you brightly wish friends and acquaintances 'Happy New Year', ask yourself exactly what you mean. What would make your year truly happy – good health, £1 million, world peace?

Keying in the word 'happiness' on the internet search engine Google yields more than three million results. These include the World Database of Happiness, a register run by Ruut Veenhoven, a professor at the University of Utrecht and the Erasmus University, Rotterdam, which lists 3,500 academic studies, 1,900 international surveys and 522 different indicators of contentment.

A study by Boots last year showed that people with high levels of wellbeing visit their doctor less often, while American research has revealed that people who consider themselves to be highly optimistic live, on average, 7.5 years longer than pessimists.

American research has revealed that people who consider themselves to be highly optimistic live, on average, 7.5 years longer than pessimists

'There is obviously something physiological going on here, but nobody has yet fully explained it,' says Dr David Peters, director of the School of Integrated Health at the University of Westminster and consultant to Boots' Wellbeing 2002 study. 'Pessimists have higher levels of most diseases, from heart disease to migraine, probably because they have an overcharged autonomic nervous system and a relatively rundown immune system. Being optimistic, which is strongly

By Barbara Lantin

associated with a high wellbeing score, has an impact on one's way of handling stress, and that affects the way our cardiovascular, nervous and immune systems work, all of which adds up to greater resilience to disease. Altering your psychological characteristics can probably increase longevity. If optimism were a drug, we would all prescribe it.'

The World Database summarises happiness as 'a subjective appreciation of life as a whole' or how well one likes the life one lives. It is not about being jolly all the time, having lots of fun or avoiding unhappy events, says Ben Renshaw, co-founder of the Happiness Project, which runs courses and workshops. 'Many people confuse pleasure with happiness. Pleasure is the next pay cheque, the next holiday, chocolates and wine. You can be a pleasure junkie, always seeking the next fix,

but all these experiences come and go. Contentment is longer term – being satisfied with your home, your job, your partner. But there's another kind of happiness that we call joy. It is not an emotion: it is a way of being, a state of mind that is available to everybody. It is not found in things: it is found in us. Just as the sun is always shining somewhere but we don't see it, so life's experiences and our limiting beliefs cloud the happiness that we were born with.'

Things that give life meaning and purpose increase your chances of being happy today

So what determines whether an individual is likely to be happy?

Research at the University of Minnesota showed that identical twins raised apart shared the same happiness level, no matter what their circumstances.

The Wellbeing survey identified 15 interrelated factors. 'When people have wellbeing, they have a feeling of being broadly in control of their lives, of being able to shape the direction their lives take,' says Dr Michelle Harrison of the Henley Centre, who analysed the data. 'They are able to manage and benefit from the increasing number of choices that life offers and they can cope with the recognition that there are parts that cannot be controlled.'

The social psychologist Professor Michael Argyle found that happy people were more likely to have at least one close relationship and a network of friends, satisfying and challenging work, absorbing leisure activities and a particular personality type.

So what determines whether an individual has a positive outlook on life? 'Things that give life meaning and purpose increase your chances of being happy today,' says psychiatrist Dr Larry Culliford. 'This includes feeling connected to others and having an active spiritual or religious life. Living in the present is also a factor, rather than dwelling on past loss or on a real or imagined future.'

'The relationship you have with yourself will determine the relationship you have with happiness'

Dr David Peters' 12 positive steps

- Eat well and stop smoking
- Take more exercise
- Learn to relax – try yoga, aromatherapy, massage or a relaxation tape
- Learn to manage stress
- Try some exercises to raise self-esteem, such as repeating positive affirmations ('I can organise my life', 'I am well loved') or setting yourself a small and realistic goal every day
- Encourage positive emotions and banish negative ones. Look on the bright side, and try to recall and re-experience times when you felt happy, relaxed and full of energy
- Communicate well with others. They will respond better and your self-esteem will grow
- Nurture your self-confidence and don't be harsh on yourself
- Express your feelings, show you care and let those close to you know how much you love them
- Make space for things that you find uplifting – art, nature, music. Drop the past, stop planning the future and notice the moment
- Be generous, unselfish and compassionate. Altruism is good for your health and hostility is bad
- Count your blessings at the end of each day

The typical happy personality is extrovert, confident and assertive, with good social skills. Happy people tend to be psychologically resilient; they remember good things about the past and are optimistic about the future. They are tolerant, with moderate views. When things go wrong, they do not blame themselves, nor set themselves unrealistic goals.

'The relationship you have with yourself will determine the relationship you have with happiness,' says Renshaw. 'Happiness is far more accessible if you have high self-esteem than if you are constantly putting yourself down and seeing yourself in a negative light.'

Money does not generally buy happiness. However, a windfall of £1 million can turn an averagely content person into a very happy one. But the good news is that although your happiness quotient may be influenced by your genes and upbringing, it can be changed for the better. Helping people to cope with life events and with stress, to feel more in control and to develop their self-esteem improves their happiness.

- The Happiness Project, tel: 01865 244414, or see www.happiness.co.uk; *Happiness – The 30-Day Guide that will Last You a Lifetime*, by Patrick Whiteside (Dr Larry Culliford's pen name), Rider, £5.99; *The Secrets of Happiness*, by Ben Renshaw, Vermilion, £4.99 (published on 6 February); *Liberation*, by the Barefoot Doctor, Element, £14.99

© Telegraph Group Limited, London 2003

Insecurity and low self-esteem . . .

. . . and how they relate to self-confidence

Most people know what insecurity and low self-esteem and feel like, but how are they different to self confidence, self belief or self love? I don't know about you, but my insecurity increases when I hear all these confusing words! This is what the Penguin *Psychology Dictionary* has to say about insecurity, low self-esteem and other similar things . . .

Self-esteem:
The degree to which one values oneself.

Insecurity:
A lack of assurance, uncertainty, unprotectedness.

Self-confidence:
Assuredness and self-reliance.

Self-belief:
Faith in one's intrinsic competence.

Self-love:
Any extreme form of love of oneself!

Self-image:
One's impression of oneself, often unconscious.

So, insecurity is about uncertainty! But surely you can't escape that? Tolerating uncertainty, or insecurity is a wonderful skill to have. However, focusing on insecurity makes you feel more insecure! (Confusing isn't it?)

Does all this complication help 'low self-esteem'?
There is so much 'out there' about this sort of thing, it can damage your self-esteem just reading about it! Here are a few questions you can think about to help clear things up a bit . . .
- Do people with high self-esteem value themselves all the time?
- Do 'secure' people never feel uncertain?
- Does having great self-confidence mean you never rely on others?
- If you have self-belief, can you never doubt yourself?
- Is 'self-love' good or bad?

I think, and it's just my opinion, that the self-help movement has left us expecting unrealistic things. Of course everyone has a feeling of insecurity at times. Everyone doubts their abilities on occasion. And the key to beating low self-esteem is not

to go around frantically thinking great things about yourself all the time.

If you expect to feel great about yourself all the time, then you will be disappointed. If you allow for the fact that sometimes you'll feel low and just let it pass, it won't last as long and you won't feel as bad.

Insecurity and low self-esteem: the biggest mistake people make!
Anything which increases the focus on the self (poor self-help books for example) makes it less likely that we will be successful in developing self-confidence or a good self-image. In a social situation, for example, self-consciousness is the opposite of what we need.

What we need is a way out of the trap, a way of building self confidence that doesn't involve increasing our self-consciousness. If you think now about the times you have really enjoyed yourself, felt particularly calm in a situation, or performed really well, I think you will find that those are times when you weren't really aware of yourself at all!

I'M SO EMBARRASSED, MY TALK WENT SO BADLY. WISH THE GROUND SWALLOWED ME UP...

BUT – IT'LL BE OLD HISTORY BY TOMORROW

This is what we are going for: rather than holding yourself in high esteem, self-acceptance can allow you to just get on with it and to enjoy doing whatever you need to do.

Beat insecurity with the self-confidence course

That is what the Self-Confidence and Low Self-Esteem Course is about. And it's free too. Six weekly email tutorials will lead you through a series of exercises, give you facts and helpful quotes. You will learn how to build self-confidence and feel good about yourself and your abilities in ways that will serve you well for the rest of your life. Once you become expert at improving self-confidence, so many

> *What we need is a way out of the trap, a way of building self-confidence that doesn't involve increasing our self consciousness*

things in life become easy and fun! We don't promise to erase insecurity, but you can get better at tolerating uncertainty!
- Our Self-Confidence Trainer CD pack is not free, but it contains many powerful exercises and

hypnotic techniques which will do their work without increasing your self-consciousness. You can also get 20% off by signing up for the free Self-Confidence Course – they work really well together. Hundreds of people have used it with remarkable results and if you want, you can order it right now – you'll be so glad you did! There's no need to suffer with a lack of self-confidence, insecurity or low self-esteem any longer.

■ The above information is from Uncommon Knowledge's web site which can be found at www.self-confidence.co.uk

© Uncommon Knowledge Ltd

Self-esteem and college

Information from the University of Cambridge Counselling Service

Self-esteem is an opinion not a fact. The way we view and feel about ourselves has a profound effect on how we live our lives. These opinions are shaped by experiences in the family, at school, from friendships and in wider society. Self-esteem involves our ability to think, to deal with life and to be happy.

The background

From infancy we look for encouragement and approval. Yet our culture does not readily give this. Parents can be tough taskmasters in seeking the best for their children, as many of you may know. Young people have a tendency to be intolerant of

difference and often mock their peers who are clever or hard working. The educational system with its emphasis on league tables implicitly demands more and more and leaves less scope for valuing improvement. There is a constant bombardment of messages telling us we should be young, slim, beautiful, fashionably dressed, have a lover and money to spend. Personal acknowledgement of ability and pride in oneself can be regarded as being arrogant, boastful, or conceited.

Rejection at any age is likely to undermine self-esteem. Events like parents separating, a boy or girlfriend being unfaithful, being ostracised by friends or picked on by peers, dealing with an unsuccessful application, having an accident, a burglary, or coping with a death are likely to provoke feelings of loss and threat. For some this is temporary, while for others the effects are long-lasting.

Conversely, success is a great ego booster, and academic achievement is an obvious source of success. However, the wealth of talent and competitive environment of Cambridge can easily lead to self-doubt and insecurity. There is a lot of pressure on students to do well for the sake of parents, college, and the

University. In fact, you may even feel that other people overestimate your ability and this burden of expectation can lead to a sense of failure and impossibility.

However, what we feel about ourselves is not based solely on what we do, it usually involves our relationships with others and whether we feel worthwhile as people. We need to be wanted, noticed, and included. We want to contribute, be of value, and make a difference – in other words to matter.

Our self-esteem continually fluctuates and is affected by events and encounters with other people. We are also constantly judging and evaluating ourselves, often in comparison with others. Observing ourselves in relation to other people can be a helpful source of learning and feedback. Yet all too often comparison slips into competition and others become a yardstick by which we evaluate ourselves as good or bad, competent or inadequate.

The reality is we are all different. Each of us has strengths and limitations which we need to learn about and learn to live with. There are aspects of our behaviour and appearance we may seek to change or develop, but a sense of self is also based on self-awareness and self-acceptance.

Suggestions for increasing self-esteem

Change is not easy. It means stepping into the unknown and taking a risk. Inevitably this means that some initiatives will work well while others don't work out as you hoped. But you can help yourself by being realistic in your choices and seeing each success as a step in the right direction.

Remember that small changes add up. Call on other people to help you by being encouraging, taking an interest, giving feedback, and making suggestions.

Do things for pleasure, for fun

- Think about ways you enjoy yourself. Put effort into making life pleasurable and satisfying. Arrange to be in situations which are playful and make you laugh.
- Learn something new. Maybe something you have always wanted to try, even something you never thought you could do. If you are stuck for ideas look on notice boards and in local publications, observe or ask other people, think about what you have enjoyed in the past.

Look after yourself physically

- Eating regularly, thinking about the sort of food you eat, and making sure you try to get the amount of sleep you need.
- Exercise and toning muscles can give confidence and help you to feel good about your body. Pay attention to how you stand and walk. Think tall.
- Pay more attention to your appearance. Pamper yourself. Choose a new hairstyle or colour in clothing. Buy a magazine which gives advice on personal presentation.

Use rewards, but avoid punishments

- Reward yourself in other ways. What about giving yourself one day off from work a week? Buy yourself a little treat. Do something you particularly enjoy but don't often get round to.

- We do not like other people saying nasty things about us so why say them to yourself? Listen to how you treat yourself – the internal conversation. Low self-esteem makes it difficult to identify strong points but it does not mean you do not have them – only that they are unfamiliar to you.
- Avoid as much as possible situations and people that leave you feeling bad about yourself and spend more time concentrating on experiences which are likely to be successful and rewarding.

Cultivate good relationships – with yourself and others

- Can you bear to be ordinary? Are you continually expecting more of yourself than you do of others? If you accept the troubles, mistakes and variability of other people, how about being happy with 'good enough' in relation to yourself?
- Involve others. Ask for support, feed-back, affection. Be prepared to say you don't know. Talk about yourself. Do not pretend or hide.

It is no good waiting for others or circumstances to leave us feeling better about ourselves. So accept responsibility for your own actions

---

Take care not to push other people away through being negative about yourself.

- Join in with others. Do not assume you are not important; other people have an effect on you and you affect them. Most people are interested in making new friends, and friendships can begin at any time in life. Say hello; do not wait for other people to come to you. Smile. Be nice to others, volunteer, be helpful, pay compliments.

Take responsibility

- It is no good waiting for others or circumstances to leave us feeling better about ourselves. So accept responsibility for your own actions: as we cannot make other people change, we need to make the changes ourselves.

If you get stuck or find it impossible to know where to start with these suggestions, maybe you can talk it through with a friend or family member, or someone else you trust. Some of the other leaflets in this series, or the self-help books listed on the Counselling Service web site (www.counselling.cam.ac.uk/booklist.html), or materials in our Resources Room may be useful. You are also welcome to talk this over with one of our counsellors.

■ The above information is from the University of Cambridge Counselling Service's web site which can be found at www.counselling.cam.ac.uk

© University of Cambridge Counselling Service

The true meaning of self-esteem

Information from the National Association for Self-Esteem (NASE)

By Robert Reasoner

Educators, parents, business and government leaders agree that we need to develop individuals with healthy or high self-esteem characterised by tolerance and respect for others, individuals who accept responsibility for their actions, have integrity, take pride in their accomplishments, who are self-motivated, willing to take risks, capable of handling criticism, loving and lovable, seek the challenge and stimulation of worthwhile and demanding goals, and take command and control of their lives. In other words, we need to help foster the development of people who have healthy or authentic self-esteem because they trust their own being to be life-affirming, constructive, responsible and trustworthy.

Unfortunately, efforts to convey the significance and critical nature of self-esteem have been hampered by misconceptions and confusion over what is meant by the term 'self-esteem'. Some have referred to self-esteem as merely 'feeling good' or having positive feelings about oneself. Others have gone so far as to equate self-esteem with egotism, arrogance, conceit, narcissism, a sense of superiority, and a trait leading to violence. Such characteristics cannot be attributed to authentic, healthy self-esteem,

because they are actually defensive reactions to the lack of authentic self-esteem, which is sometimes referred to as 'pseudo self-esteem'.

Individuals with defensive or low self-esteem typically focus on trying to prove themselves or impress others. They tend to use others for their own gain. Some act with arrogance and contempt towards others. They generally lack confidence in themselves, often have doubts about their worth and acceptability, and hence are reluctant to take risks or expose themselves to failure. They frequently blame others for their shortcomings rather than take responsibility for their actions.

A close relationship has been documented between low self-esteem and such problems as violence, alcoholism, drug abuse, eating disorders, school dropouts, teenage pregnancy, suicide, and low academic achievement. However, it has been difficult to isolate it as a primary cause using traditional experimental research methods, for it is usually only one of several contributing factors. What needs to be stressed is that self-esteem is a critical component of any programme aimed at self-improvement or any rehabilitation programme, for it is one of the few solutions that offers hope to correcting these problems. Many prisons, for example, have now introduced self-esteem programmes to reduce recidivism.

One of the difficulties in trying to reach agreement

on the nature of self-esteem is due to the fact that it has been approached from several different perspectives. Some have seen it as a psycho-dynamic, developmental process; others have approached it from the perspective of the cognitive-behaviourist in terms of various coping strategies; others have viewed it from the position of a social psychologist in terms of attitudes, while others have focused on the experiential dimensions of self-esteem as a humanistic psychologist. Since self-esteem has both psychological and sociological dimensions, this has made it difficult to come up with a comprehensive definition, and rarely have both dimensions been taken into consideration together in conducting research studies.

> *Since self-esteem has both psychological and sociological dimensions, this has made it difficult to come up with a comprehensive definition*

There is, however, general agreement that the term self-esteem includes cognitive, affective, and behavioural elements. It is cognitive as one consciously thinks about oneself as one considers the discrepancy between one's ideal self, the person one wishes to be, and the perceived self or the realistic appraisal of how one sees oneself. The affective element refers to the feelings or emotions that one has when considering that discrepancy. The behavioural aspects of self-esteem are manifested in such behaviours as assertiveness, resilience, being

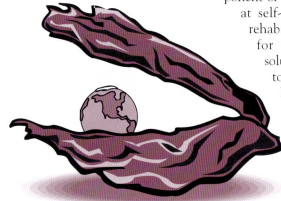

decisive and respectful of others. Thus, self-esteem is difficult to define because of these multiple dimensions. In addition, although self-esteem is generally stable, it can fluctuate from time to time, a phenomenon which is referred to as global versus situational self-esteem, and which can make measuring or researching self-esteem very difficult.

It is important that the significance of self-esteem not be lost in the confusion over what it means. Nathaniel Branden, PhD, a well-known psychotherapist, defined self-esteem several years ago as 'The disposition to experience oneself as being competent to cope with the basic challenges of life and of being worthy of happiness.' The National Association for Self-Esteem modified this to define self-esteem as 'The experience of being capable of meeting life's challenges and being worthy of happiness.' Christopher Mruk, PhD, a psychology professor at Bowling Green University, reports in his book *Self-Esteem: Research, Theory, and Practice* that of all the theories and definitions proposed, this description of self-esteem has best withstood the test of time in terms of accuracy and comprehensiveness.

A strong sense of worthiness prevents competence from becoming arrogance by keeping the individual focused on basic values

This concept of self-esteem is founded on the premise that it is strongly connected to a sense of competence and worthiness and the relationship between the two as one lives life. The worthiness component of self-esteem is often misunderstood as simply feeling good about oneself, when it actually is tied to whether or not a person lives up to certain fundamental human values, such as finding meanings that foster human growth and making commitments to them in a way that leads to a sense of

GOAL

integrity and satisfaction. A sense of competence is having the conviction that one is generally capable of producing desired results, having confidence in the efficacy of our mind and our ability to think, as well as to make appropriate choices and decisions. Worthiness might be considered the psychological aspect of self-esteem, while competence might be considered the behavioural or sociological aspect of self-esteem. Self-esteem stems from the experience of living consciously and might be viewed as a person's overall judgement of himself or herself pertaining to self-competence and self-worth based on reality.

The value of this definition is that it is useful in making the distinction between authentic or healthy self-esteem and pseudo or unhealthy self-esteem. A sense of personal worth without competence is just as limiting as competence without worthiness. A strong sense of worthiness prevents competence from becoming arrogance by keeping the individual focused on basic values, and competence prevents worthiness from becoming narcissism by requiring good feelings to be earned, not given. Thus, behaviours that might be described as egotistic, egocentric, conceited, boasting or bragging, bullying, taking advantage of, or harming others are defensive behaviours indicative of a lack of self-esteem. Such behaviours, therefore, should not be confused with authentic, healthy self-esteem.

Unfortunately, some of the confusion over the term self-esteem

has stemmed from programmes and strategies used that were not grounded in sound research. Such strategies include heaping children with undeserved praise not based on accomplishment. Most feel that it is critical that any efforts to build self-esteem be grounded in reality. It cannot be attained by merely reciting boosters or affirmations, and one cannot give others authentic self-esteem. To do so is likely to result in an inflated sense of worth. Most feel that a sense of competence is strengthened through realistic and accurate self-appraisal, meaningful accomplishments, overcoming adversities, bouncing back from failures, and adopting practices such as assuming self-responsibility and maintaining integrity which engender one's sense of competence and self-worth.

We don't believe that it is possible to have too much true self-esteem, for having high self-esteem is equivalent to having good health

Is it possible to have too much self-esteem? We don't believe that it is possible to have too much true self-esteem, for having high self-esteem is equivalent to having good health. However, it is certainly possible for individuals to have an over-inflated sense of either worth or competence. Our objective is to develop individuals with high self-esteem that is well grounded in reality and balanced between an equal sense of worth and competence – individuals who exhibit those qualities agreed upon by educators, parents, business and government leaders as essential to effective functioning in these changing times.

■ The above information is from the National Association for Self-Esteem's (NASE) web site which can be found at www.self-esteem-nase.org

© *National Association for Self-Esteem (NASE)*

Self-esteem or self-confidence

Undertaking a successful self-development programme

D o you find it hard to get your ideas across at work? You have lots of them, often really good ones, but somehow your quiet way puts you at a disadvantage. People with low self-confidence or self-esteem can miss out on hot opportunities because they don't put themselves forward when these opportunities come round. Very often the fear that underlies this is that you are afraid of being accused of grabbing the limelight, that you'll be thought of as pushy and unpleasant, and that other people won't like you. These are powerful reasons for remaining self-effacing, but there are other ways to deal with this chronic lack of self-confidence and it is becoming increasingly important to do so.

The real thing

No doubt you know people who seem to be truly confident and at ease. Bear in mind that you can discount this appearance with many people. A great many people pretend confidence very convincingly but their insides don't match their outsides. Within they are quivering, just waiting to be spotted as the fraud they feel like, but on the outside

By Elizabeth Morris MA (Psych), MAHPP. Buckholdt Associates

they are calm and confident. This is a very stressful way to go through each day and this stress can take its toll over time, resulting in ill health. These people are not displaying much Emotional Intelligence. Nevertheless there are people around who aren't just pretending – but really are centred in themselves, not over-confident and cocky, but quietly powerful. They command respect, they are knowledgeable, modest yet assured and most of all they get listened to. What they say counts,

> *A great many people pretend confidence very convincingly but their insides don't match their outsides. Within they are quivering*

people get excited about their suggestions. They think of these people first when a new project is proposed at management level. These confident people inspire confidence from other people too. They are seen as having 'safe hands'. This person has both sound self-esteem and plenty of self-confidence – it is the combination that gives them such a powerful presence. These people are truly Emotionally Intelligent. Building your self-confidence will certainly help you improve your Emotional Intelligence and this article will outline some tips for creating your own self-development plan.

Some little-known facts about self-confidence

1. Self-esteem is not the same as self-confidence

Self-esteem is the feeling we have about our worth and value as a person.

Self-confidence is the feeling we have about our ability to do things.

In other words esteem is about your 'being' and confidence is about what you 'do'. Knowing the difference means that you don't try to build your confidence when it's

really your self-esteem that needs a hand. Many people are confident about their ability to drive a car, go on a course or bake a cake, but fewer are sure that they are valuable, worthwhile human beings who bring something special and unique to the world.

Can you identify which you need most? Check with yourself. Do you know that you are valued and loved for WHO you are? Do you have people in your life who care about you no matter what? If you don't have this sense of being accepted and loved it can be hard to feel loving of yourself and your self-esteem may be low. Do you feel confident about your abilities in certain areas? Do you think of yourself as a person who can tackle many things and expect to be reasonably successful at them? Or do you think that you will have a hard time learning something new? If this is what you think about yourself your self-confidence is likely to be low.

Obviously both self-esteem and self-confidence impact on one another, but the real key is to have strong self-esteem. This will allow you to take risks and try new things and not be knocked if you don't succeed immediately.

If you want to build your self-esteem the first thing to do is to identify your Self-Esteem Building Team. Who are the people who love you just the way you are, who don't need you to be achieving and doing all kinds of clever things to get their approval? Once you have identified who these people are (one or two is enough) ask them to help you work on this self-development project. They then become your supporters and champions and will send you cards with encouraging messages, leave supportive words on your answerphone, surprise you with a fun trip because they love you . . . Your job is to open yourself up to the messages your Team are sending you. Very often we don't notice the loving acceptance that is already around us, but when we start to pay attention we can absorb it, like a sponge soaking up warm and soothing water. That is the beginning of being able to feel that way about ourselves and having sound self-esteem.

Obviously both self-esteem and self-confidence impact on one another, but the real key is to have strong self-esteem

---

2. The self-confidence spiral

There is a psychological law that seems to operate with our inner thoughts and feelings. If we think negative thoughts about ourselves we will spiral down, feeling worse and worse. If we think positively about ourselves we get onto an upwards spiral. We build better and better feelings about ourselves because after we feel good we tend to do well, when we do well we feel good about ourselves and so on. We can use the knowledge of these spirals to help ourselves.

Try casting your mind back to a time when you were feeling good about yourself. Remember how you felt, how your body reacted to this, you may have felt light and free, happy and warm. Think about how you held your body then, did you laugh and smile? Now remember a time when you felt low and really lacking in self-belief. What did your body feel like then? Practise moving from one state to the other just by changing your body posture and mind set.

3. Being self-confident doesn't mean not feeling nervous; think about it

Being truly self-confident means being honest, at least to yourself, about how nervous you really are.

If you let yourself or a friend know how you feel you will be able to work out what you need to support you as you tackle the scary situation. This increases the chances of you being successful and so boosting you store of confidence even more. In the same way as you can have a Self-Esteem Building Team supporting you, you can have the Self Confidence Booster Club. If a group of you get together and commit to supporting each other, this can be very helpful as you prepare to tackle new projects and develop your skills – and therefore your confidence.

Changing your negative self-beliefs

Just imagine you are walking out of the office at your lunch break, a group of you together, talking and laughing. What's happening in your head? Is the little voice saying"
- No one wants to walk with me.
- John's always so popular.
- This is just like at school.
- Jean's going to get promoted again.
- Look at how he sweet-talks the manager.
- Why doesn't she ever listen to me like that?
- I must be really stupid.
- What must he think of me?
- I don't have to bother to impress them.
- This is nothing to do with me, I'm accounts not sales.
- I don't know anything about this so what I have to say is irrelevant.

That stream of criticism can just go on and on. Sometimes you direct it at yourself and sometimes at other people. The more you direct the criticism at yourself the more of a threat it is for you to act confidently and assertively. Whereas the more you direct it at other people the more of a threat it is to do anything because you're running such a hard comparison in your mind. Your fear is that one day you'll be the one to come off badly in the comparison.

What to do next

When you've identified those negative thoughts and written them down the next thing you need to do is make a column next to that list and fill in a set of positive things you could say instead that counteract the first ones. For instance 'John's always so popular' – the sub-text to this is – 'and I'm not', so think of times when you have been in a group and had people listening to you, or wanting to talk to you. It may only have been once before, it may only have been a long time ago – it doesn't matter. The important thing is that it disproves the thing you are undermining yourself with – and reminds you of an alternative. If you tend to think really negative things about other people try the following: 'Look at the way he's sweet-talking the manager – what a creep!' Followed by – 'I'm going to watch to see if he gets what he wants from that approach – and if he does I'll try something similar.'

The next thing to do is NOT to try to stop yourself from doing this negative chattering. That may surprise you but what I want you to do instead is increase the amount of praise you give yourself and other people. Praise yourself quietly internally and other people out loud. Of course if you are relaxed enough to praise yourself out loud too, that's great, go ahead and do it, but it's going to work just fine if you do it silently to yourself.

Daydream your way to reality

Use your imagination and transport yourself forward in time until you can see exactly what a day or a week in the life of a self-confident you at work would look like. What would you be doing, how would you be acting, what would other people be saying to you, how would you look, what would you be wearing, what position would you hold? Really go for it and picture the whole scene in as much detail as

---

If we think negative thoughts about ourselves we will spiral down, feeling worse and worse. If we think positively about ourselves we get onto an upwards spiral

---

Three tips that are worth remembering

Any self-development programme takes time to show results. We have usually taken a long time to develop the habits we are trying to break and we need a bit of time and some encouragement to change them to more effective new ones. So remember that:

– Things need to be tried more than once
– If you are changing your behaviour other people will take a while to respond
– Don't give up until you've given it at least 20 – yes, 20! – tries

The three main causes for lack of confidence at work

There are three main causes for lack of confidence at work:
1 Lack of self-esteem.
2 The way we daily, sometimes even hourly, defeat ourselves through our negative self-beliefs.
3 Being bullied by someone else. (If this is happening to you get help as soon as possible. You do not deserve that treatment and the bully must be stopped.)

possible, right down to the office you'd have, or the car, or the clothes you'll be wearing. Keep this image in your mind, write it down, draw it, pin it up on the fridge, paste it into your diary. Look at it often. Then get yourself a buddy or mentor and sit down with

them regularly to get down a set of goals to achieve so that this image of yourself becomes reality. You must take action every day – even if it is only a small thing.

■ Elizabeth Morris is an organisational psychologist and registered psychotherapist. She and her partner, Tim Sparrow, created Buckholdt Associates, a human performance consultancy specialising in Emotional Intelligence assessment and development. She has written many Emotional Intelligence programmes, working with a wide variety of organisations such as banks, manufacturing companies, IT organisations and schools. The University of Bristol is currently running their programmes on Emotional Intelligence and Self-Motivation, Emotional Coaching and Beating Workplace Bullying. The Centre for British Teachers runs their programmes on Building Self-Esteem in the Classroom, which is Elizabeth's personal passion. She is a director of the Centre for Applied Emotional Intelligence, an organisation that provides professional training programmes for EI practitioners.

■ Self-Esteem Advisory Service, Buckholdt House, The Street, Frampton On Severn, Gloucestershire, GL2 7ED. Tel: + 44 (0)1452 741106 Fax: + 44 (0)1452 741520. Web: www.buckholdtassociates.com

© Buckholdt Associates

Adolescence – a time of crisis in self-esteem

*By Robert W. Reasoner,
President, International
Council for Self-Esteem*

Today's youth face a far different and far more competitive world than their parents and grandparents. With unlimited information at their fingertips and extraordinary opportunities waiting to be tapped, they must possess a body of knowledge that is both broad and deep. They must know how to think critically, to solve complex problems, to work in teams and adapt to rapidly changing technology. They must be lifelong learners to keep up with the body of knowledge which now doubles every two or three years. This requires individuals who possess healthy, high self-esteem.

Yet, studies indicate that youth, and especially adolescents, are riddled with self-doubt about who they are and how they feel about themselves. This has been found to be true for 60% of those between the ages of 12 and 17. In grade 4 or age 9-10, 65% of both boys and girls report feeling good about themselves. However, during adolescence many experience a significant decline in self-esteem. Studies have indicated that 85% can identify ways they would like to improve. The level of self-esteem of girls drops to as low as 29% by age 17 and to 45% for boys.

Why is this? Children base their level of self-esteem primarily upon the feedback they receive from their parents and other significant adults

Studies indicate that youth, and especially adolescents, are riddled with self-doubt about who they are and how they feel about themselves

in their lives. However, as they enter adolescence young people begin to use other criteria upon which to base their self-esteem. Instead of relying on their parents for feedback or focusing on their qualities of integrity, a strong sense of values, or their personal growth and accomplishments, they begin to look to their peers for acceptance and positive feedback. Many become concerned about their appearance in a media-saturated world that emphasises good looks. This is especially true for girls. They internalise the messages and expectations they have received from the media and try to keep up with the impossible demands of this unrealistic image. Only 4 out of every 10 teenage girls consider themselves attractive. One-half of adolescent girls want to lose weight. This often leads to the eating disorders of anorexia nervosa and bulimia and lower self-esteem.

Adolescence can also be a time of crisis for boys, who begin to base their self-esteem on their body image and their athletic prowess. A recent study indicated that half the boys want to tone up physically. They strive to excel in competitive sports and seek ways to become stronger or faster. Being good in art or music or strong academically isn't nearly as important to them as being popular and a good athlete. Unfortunately, as they approach adulthood they find out that these qualities are not those that lead to success in life.

Adolescents with low self-esteem typically suffer from a crisis of self-confidence that is manifested through a variety of behaviours. Those with low self-esteem typically find it important to prove themselves to others and seek ways to compensate for these feelings of low self-esteem. They can be observed either withdrawing from social contacts or attempting to prove their significance by showing off, engaging in risky behaviour, bullying others, or developing notions of grandiosity to compensate for their low self-esteem. They are easily influenced or manipulated by others. Some strive to be popular and engage in various behaviours to gain favour with their peers, using alcohol or drugs, or even engaging in delinquent behaviour or unsafe sex.

Only 4 out of every 10 teenage girls consider themselves attractive. One-half of adolescent girls want to lose weight

They have more psychological problems, poor academic records, diminished peer support and increased depression. They suffer from insecurity, negative moods, feelings of inadequacy, and often feel trapped in a self-image of failure. Their behaviour is likely to become anti-social; they treat others poorly, and exhibit impatience and hostility towards others.

What can adolescents do to avoid feelings of low self-esteem? First, they need to be aware of the pitfalls of striving too hard to base their self-esteem on being popular or seeking the approval of others. Research has shown that boys who tended to be observers, calm, socially at ease, and satisfied with themselves at age 14 experienced continued growth in self-esteem and became more successful as adults. Girls described as moralistic, sympathetic, considerate, and sought out by friends for advice reported gains in self-esteem between the ages of 18 and 23. Thus, those that focus primarily on internal factors, becoming the kind of person they want to be, and basing their behaviour on their personal values, and exhibiting the behaviours they feel good about end up feeling best about themselves as adults.

The best way to sustain a self-esteem is not to seek the approval of others but to acquire and demonstrate competence by gaining new skills and making progress towards one's goals. When individuals set meaningful and realistic goals and see themselves as making growth or achieving those goals, they experience increased self-esteem. Engaging in activities that benefit others, including tutoring young people, bringing help or pleasure to seniors, or working to improve the quality of the community are ways to build positive feelings about oneself.

© International Council for Self-Esteem

How to . . . increase your self-esteem

How can I build up my self-esteem?

Take care of your physical health. Make sure you have good food, relaxation and enough sleep. Try to make sure that you have 10-15 minutes of moderate exercise (e.g. brisk walking) every day, and about 20 minutes of more vigorous exercise three times a week (something that raises your heartbeat and makes you sweat). Have a massage whenever you can. Nothing is better for increasing self-esteem and beating stress! Learn to recognise your own stress indicators, and when they occur, take time out to look after yourself.

Avoid whenever possible, situations where you have little power, and institutions that undermine your self-esteem.
This may be difficult or appear impossible in the short run, but may be essential to your long-term mental and physical wellbeing. De-stress your home as much as possible: make sure it is as tidy as suits you, with good lighting and supportive seating.

Set yourself a challenge that you can realistically achieve, and then go for it! Start with something relatively small, such as, 'Getting fit enough to walk up the steps to my flat without getting out of breath or taking the lift'. (But not 'Running the Marathon this year' unless, of course, that is a realistic goal for you!) Then, when you have achieved

---

Written by Penny Cloutte

---

it, reward yourself! Tell your friends, and let them praise you for it. Then set yourself another challenge. Learn to enjoy your own achievements.

Learn something new. It doesn't really matter what it is, whether it's car maintenance, or speaking Russian or flower arranging. The important thing is that it interests you and will give you a sense of achievement. The longer you have been away from learning something new, and the more different the new subject is from your normal life, the more benefit this will give you! For example, if you are an intellectual sort of person, take up weight training or yoga. If you are a handy, craftsman-like person, try and learn a foreign language, or teach yourself a new style of dance . . .

Find out what you most enjoy, and then find ways of doing it as much as possible. If you enjoy it, you probably have some talent for it, whatever it is. Doing what we are best at is the most empowering and self-nourishing kind of activity.

Join in with others, if possible, to take action about the things that annoy you – whether it's the amount of dog mess in your street, government policy on asylum-seekers, the world-wide arms trade, or whatever most angers you. Of course, the trick here is to find the right group of fellow-campaigners, a group where you feel respected and empowered. Unfortunately, political campaigning groups can be as damaging to the self-esteem of their members as other kinds of institutions! This is perhaps an area where continuing struggle is not only necessary, but a sign of love for oneself, one's fellow-humans and for the world.

Give yourself regular treats, to remind yourself that you deserve nurture and pleasure. Programme some fun into your plans for each week, to nurture your sense of humour and creativity.

Learn to sing! To free your voice is empowering to mind, soul and body. Singing strengthens the lungs and the legs, gives joy and hope, and is a powerful medium for self-expression. You can do it alone, or as part of a group. Many places now have 'Choirs for the Tone Deaf' or 'Can't Sing' groups which take on the fact that many of us may have had painful experiences with music teachers in the past. They can teach ways of addressing this, involving breath and relaxation techniques.

■ Reprinted from *How to . . . increase your self-esteem* by permission of Mind (National Association for Mental Health).

© Mind

How can I improve my self-esteem?

Information from KidsHealth

By D'Arcy Lyness, PhD

Self-esteem involves how much a person values herself and appreciates her own worth and importance. For example, a teen with healthy self-esteem is able to feel good about her character and her qualities and take pride in her abilities, skills, and accomplishments. Self-esteem is the result of comparing how we'd like to be and what we'd like to accomplish with how we actually see ourselves.

Everyone experiences problems with self-esteem at certain times in their lives – especially teens who are still figuring out who they are and where they fit into the world. How a teen feels about herself can be related to many different factors, such as her environment, her body image, her expectations of herself, and her experiences. For example, if a person has had problems in her family, has had to deal with difficult relationships, or sets unrealistic standards for herself, this can lead to low self-esteem.

Recognising that you can improve your self-esteem is a great first step in doing so. Learning what can hurt self-esteem and what can build it is also important. Then, with a little effort, a person can really improve the way she feels about herself.

Constant criticism can harm self-esteem – and it doesn't always come from others! Some teens have an 'inner critic', a voice inside that seems to find fault with everything they do – and self-esteem obviously has a hard time growing in such an environment. Some people have modelled their inner critic's voice

> *Everyone experiences problems with self-esteem at certain times in their lives – especially teens who are still figuring out who they are and where they fit into the world*

after a critical parent or teacher whose acceptance was important to them. The good news is that this inner critic can be retrained, and because it now belongs to you, you can be the one to decide that the inner critic will only give constructive feedback from now on.

It may help to pinpoint any unrealistic expectations that may be affecting your self-esteem. Do you wish you were thinner? Smarter? More popular? A better athlete? Although it's easy for teens to feel a little inadequate physically, socially, or intellectually, it's also important to recognise what you can change and what you can't, and to aim for accomplishments rather than perfection. You may wish to be a star athlete, but it may be more realistic to set your sights on improving your game in specific ways this season. If you are thinking about your shortcomings, try to start thinking about other positive aspects of yourself that outweigh them. Maybe you're not the tallest person in your class and maybe you're not class prefect, but you're awesome at volleyball or painting or playing the guitar.

Remember – each person excels at different things and your talents are constantly developing.

If you want to improve your self-esteem, there are some steps you can take to start empowering yourself:

- Remember that self-esteem involves much more than liking your appearance. Because of rapid changes in growth and appearance, teens often fall into the trap of believing their entire self-esteem hinges on how they look. Don't miss the inner beauty that's more than skin deep in yourself and in others.
- Think about what you're good at and what you enjoy, and build on those abilities. Take pride in new skills you develop and talents you have. Share what you can do with others.
- Exercise! You'll relieve stress, and be healthier and happier.
- Try to stop thinking negative thoughts about yourself. When you catch yourself being too critical, counter it by saying something positive about yourself.
- Take pride in your opinions and ideas – and don't be afraid to voice them.
- Each day, write down three things about yourself that make you happy.
- Set goals. Think about what you'd like to accomplish, then make a plan for how to do it. Stick with your plan and keep track of your progress. If you realise that you're unhappy with something about yourself that you can change, then start today. If it's something you can't change (like your height), then start to work toward loving yourself the way you are.
- Beware the perfectionist! Are you expecting the impossible? It's good to aim high, but your goals for yourself should be within reach.

Have fun – enjoy spending time with the people you care about and doing the things you love

- Make a contribution. Tutor a classmate who's having trouble, help clean up your neighbourhood, participate in a walk-a-thon for a good cause, the list goes on. Feeling like you're making a difference can do wonders to improve self-esteem.
- Have fun – enjoy spending time with the people you care about and doing the things you love.

It's never too late to build or improve self-esteem. In some cases, a teen may need the help of a mental health professional, like a therapist or psychologist, to help heal emotional hurt and build healthy, positive self-esteem. A therapist can help a teen to learn to love herself and realise that her differences make her unique.

So, what's the payoff? Self-esteem plays a role in almost everything you do – teens with high self-esteem do better in school and enjoy it more and find it easier to make friends. They tend to have better relationships with peers and adults, feel happier, find it easier to deal with mistakes, disappointments, and failures, and are more likely to stick with something until they succeed. Improving self-esteem takes work, but the payoff is feeling good about yourself and your accomplishments.

- This information was provided by KidsHealth, one of the largest resources online for medically reviewed health information written for parents, kids, and teens. For more articles like this one, visit www.KidsHealth.org or www.TeensHealth.org

© KidsHealth.org

Top tips to being assertive, not aggressive!

There is a huge difference between being assertive and getting what you want, and being aggressive and getting a smack in the gob. Follow our top tips to getting your point across:

1. Try not to shout, it's the easiest way to get people angry, try and keep calm and focused on the point you are trying to put across
2. Try and be as truthful as possible, lying or exaggerating will not help you.
3. Don't back down, if you are right, and someone is trying to pull a fast one on you, then stick to your guns!
4. Keep your language as clean as possible, just try to portray a strong image, going overboard on the swear words doesn't help.
5. Keep your distance from the person you are talking to, it sounds stupid but most people have an imaginary area of 'personal space' about 1 metre around them, to keep things calm it's best to keep out of it!
6. If you are asking for something, or trying to get someone to do something for you, be specific, say 'Let's meet at 8pm at mine' instead of 'let's meet sometime'.
7. If you want to disagree with someone, disagree civilly, don't just agree (or disagree) for the sake of it; be nice.
8. If you have a particular message or point to give to someone, tell it to them directly, it's best to do it face to face.
9. Try and keep your body language calm, don't wave your arms about, point or push the person(s) you're talking to, not a good move if you want to appear non-aggressive.
10. Most importantly, if you feel you are losing your cool, stop and count to 10; it sounds stupid, but it works!

- The above information is from Pupiline's web site which can be found at www.pupiline.net

© 1999-2003 Pupiline Limited

How to develop self-esteem in children

By Words of Discovery

Effects of raising self-esteem

There has been a lot of talk recently about the importance of raising children's self-esteem, but what effect does this really have on the behaviour and happiness of our children? There have been numerous studies done (a few here, many in the States) to show the positive effect that focusing on raising children's self-esteem has on children. If we examine the causes of aggression, bullying, withdrawal, failure, showing-off, etc., we discover that lack of self-esteem is at the root of this 'anti-social' behaviour. Studies show that poor school achievement, truancy, crime, violence, alcohol and drug abuse, teenage pregnancy, suicide and susceptibility to peer pressure all have strong links to poor self-esteem.

How self-esteem is developed

The main source of nurturing and development is parents. When children are born they have total self-belief. They believe they are unique, they are the most valuable being in the world. Their world revolves around them, they have a life mission which they are here to fulfil. As they grow older, and more aware of others, they have to come to terms with the fact that other people inhabit their world and have their own needs. What do we do at this time to ensure our children maintain their feeling of uniqueness?

How long does it take for a child to learn self-doubt and lose self-confidence?

Children have powerful imaginations. If a child hears: 'That's not right you silly fool', or 'Why can't you do that properly?' or 'Why do you have to be so messy?' their imagination will run a very powerful image of what they 'should' be like and contrast that with the 'silly fool/ messy/incapable/not good enough'

person that they are now. Frequent repetition of these images will result in children very quickly developing feelings of self-doubt, lack of self-worth and lack of confidence.

Raising children

We hear a lot these days about how difficult it is to raise balanced, self-motivated, positive children in today's climate of technological change and media influence. There is no doubt that the world is changing fast, but it always has, and parents have always faced challenges when raising their children. We need to feel concern about the way we nurture our children, it is only when we are conscious of what we are doing that we can pay attention to how we can build on the good practice we already have. As parents we are all doing the very best we can and it is important for us all to appreciate this. It is also important to be realistic in our expectations of ourselves and our children. How can we, as parents and teachers, empower our children to build self-esteem and achieve their potential? I believe there are four pillars of self-esteem: Belonging, Power, Role Models, Uniqueness.

Belonging

Children need to feel a sense of having a recognised place in the world, that they belong to a family, a heritage, a community and the universe. They need to have the opportunity to explore and celebrate these links. The easiest way to do this is to spend time with children doing things that they and you enjoy doing together, giving them your full attention. Loving your child abundantly and openly will develop their security and sense of belonging. In her wonderful book *Curriculum of Love – Cultivating the Spiritual Nature of Children*, Morgan Simone Daleo offers a collection of activities centred on 10 core values: harmony, awareness, selflessness, self-reliance, celebrating others, empathy, compassion, beauty, balance (body, mind and emotions) and joy. Together they form a curriculum of love to help adults creatively encourage a caring attitude in children.

Power

The development of children's inner power will happen as a consequence of raised self-esteem. By encouraging children to set goals and celebrating their achievements they will develop self-belief and the belief that what they do will make a difference to the world. Stress is a potential barrier to self-belief and realising our inner power. We all experience stress and anxiety at times and in his book *A Parenting Manual* Doc Lew Childre explains an excellent, effective and easy method to eliminate the effects of stress on your children. It is called 'Freeze-Framing' and 'it can help anyone direct their own life more intelligently'. The process of 'Freeze-Framing' enables you to recognise a stressful feeling, take time to refocus your mind and by listening to your heart and recalling a positive, fun feeling enables you to have a more efficient, controlled response to the situation. It enables you to remain calm and logical when dealing with upset and angry children and therefore resolve the situation lovingly and positively. And the process works equally well for children learning to manage stress in their relationships and develop their inner power.

Role model

Parents are the most influential role models children have. Whatever values and beliefs we want our children to learn, those are the beliefs and values we have to live our lives by. 'Do what I say, don't do what I do' does not work. We must demonstrate our values consciously in all we do and say, including respect for others and self-respect. We should also be aware that books, films and TV have an enormous influence (both positive and negative) on how children perceive themselves in their world.

Self-esteem is the greatest gift we can develop in our children because with high self-esteem anything is and will be possible. We are what we think we can be

Uniqueness

Taking the time to listen, talk to and praise our children will help develop their sense of being special. There are also a number of excellent story books available for children which celebrate uniqueness and difference and develop self-esteem and values.

Self-esteem is the greatest gift we can develop in our children because with high self-esteem anything is and will be possible. We are what we think we can be.

- Words of Discovery is the UK's only specialist in children's personal development books and books on positive parenting. To order any of the books featured here, or to request a copy of their latest catalogue, contact Words of Discovery by phone or fax on 0116 273 3000 or Freepost at: Words of Discovery, Freepost LON7858, Leicester, LE8 0JZ.

- The above information is from *Families* Magazine's web site which can be found at www.familiesmagazine.co.uk

© *Families*

Constant testing 'demotivates' pupils

Repeated testing has a detrimental effect on schoolchildren's motivation for learning, it was claimed today. A research review showed that repeated testing lowered pupils' self-esteem and started a downward spiral of lower motivation, less effort and even lowered results, according to academics at Bristol University.

Children particularly discouraged by testing were girls and low-achievers, for whom the consequences of perceived failure had a bigger impact on self-esteem.

Professor Wynne Harlen, one of the academics behind the research review, said that while there was plenty of evidence on the issue of why test results were improving, she had wanted to look at a different aspect.

'What we wanted to look at was the effect on children's motivation.

'If you think about the current policy of encouraging life-long learning and the importance of that, then one of the important things is that kids should come out of school with this motivation to learn.'

She said the review, which looked at studies carried out in Britain and abroad, found that all pointed towards a serious and negative effect on students' motivation to learn.

Professor Harlen said it was not the tests themselves but the testing culture which most affected pupils.

'With tests having what we call high stakes – in other words they are important for the school, for the teachers – teachers are not just giving the test, but also practice tests and lots of revision and so on.

'There is constant repetition. It is the testing culture rather than the tests that does it.'

According to the review, detrimental effects also include pupils seeing the goals of education in terms of passing tests rather than developing an understanding about what they are learning, and that they judge themselves and others by their test results.

A consequence is that the gap between the lower and higher achieving pupils is widened, it added.

© *Guardian Newspapers Limited 2002*

Body image and self-esteem

Information from KidsHealth

I'm fat. I'm too skinny. I'd be happy if I were taller, shorter, had curly hair, straight hair, a smaller nose, bigger muscles, longer legs. Is there something wrong with me?

Do any of these statements sound familiar? Are you used to putting yourself down? If so, you're not alone. As a teen, you're going through a ton of changes in your body, and as your body changes, so does your image of yourself. Read on to learn more about how your body image affects your self-esteem and how you can develop a healthy body image.

Why are self-esteem and body image important?

You may have heard the term self-esteem on talk shows or seen it in your favourite magazine. But what does it mean? Self-esteem involves how much a person values herself, and appreciates her own worth. Self-esteem is important because when you feel good about yourself, you enjoy life more.

Although self-esteem applies to every aspect of how you see yourself, it is often mentioned in terms of appearance or body image. Body image is how you see and feel about your physical appearance. We tend to relate self-esteem to body image for several reasons. First of all, most people care about how other people see them. Unfortunately, many people judge others by things like the clothes they wear, the shape of their body, or the way they wear their hair. If a person feels like he or she looks different from others, then body image and self-esteem may be affected negatively.

Teens with a poor body image may think negative thoughts like, 'I'm fat, I'm not pretty enough, I'm not strong enough.'

What shapes self-esteem?
The effects of puberty

Some teens struggle with their self-esteem when they begin puberty. That's because the body undergoes many changes when puberty starts. These rapid changes and the desire for acceptance make it difficult for teens to judge whether they are 'normal' when they look at other teens around them. And many people worry about what's normal during puberty. But puberty doesn't proceed at the same pace for everyone.

Puberty usually begins with a growth spurt. Usually, this happens to girls first but guys tend to catch up with their own spurts around the ages of 13 or 14. In general, puberty for both sexes takes between 2 and 5 years to complete but every teen has her own genetic timetable for the changes of puberty.

The sexual development of girls typically starts around age 9 to 10 with the appearance of budding breasts, pubic hair, and later the start of menstruation. Other changes include wider hips, buttocks and thighs, and a greater proportion of body fat. These changes can make a girl feel self-conscious about her body. She may feel like her maturing body draws attention to her, and feel uncomfortable or embarrassed. Or she may feel as though her body is weird and different from her friends' bodies. Unhealthy 'crash' dieting or eating disorders can result.

Self-esteem involves how much a person values herself, and appreciates her own worth

Meanwhile, guys will begin to notice their shoulders getting wider, muscles developing, voices deepening, testicles getting larger, and penises growing longer and wider. Guys who are dissatisfied with their development may become obsessed with weight training and may take steroids or other drugs to help boost their physiques and athletic performance.

The effects of culture

Media images from TV, movies, and advertising may affect self-esteem. Girls may struggle with media images of teen girls and women who are unrealistically thin. Many women and teen girls in magazines, the news, or on TV are unusually thin, which may lead girls who are not thin to believe that something is wrong with them. It's important to realise that self-worth should not be determined by body size. It's more important to lead a healthy lifestyle by exercising regularly and eating nutritiously than to try to change your body to fit an unrealistic ideal.

Guys can also have body image problems. Although girls may feel pressured to be smaller, guys may feel pressured to become larger and look stronger. Sports and other guys may put pressure on guys to gain muscle

mass quickly, which can lead them to feel unhappy or dissatisfied with their bodies.

Sometimes low self-esteem is too much to bear. Instead of getting help, some teens may drink or do drugs to help themselves feel better, especially in social situations.

The effects of home and school

Your home or school life may also affect your self-esteem. Some parents spend more time criticising than praising their children. Sometimes this criticism reduces a teen's ability to have a positive body image – the teen may model her own 'inner voice' after that of a parent, and learn to think negative thoughts about herself.

It's hard to succeed at school when the situation at home is tense, so sometimes teens who suffer from abuse at home may have problems in school, both of which contribute to poor self-esteem.

Teens may also experience negative comments and hurtful teasing or bullying from classmates and peers. This can definitely affect a person's self-esteem, but it's important to remember that the people who are being hurtful probably have low self-esteem as well, and putting others down may make them feel better about themselves.

Sometimes racial and ethnic prejudice is the source of hurtful comments. These comments come from ignorance on the part of the person who makes them, but sometimes they can negatively affect a person's body image and self-esteem.

Checking your own self-esteem and body image

If you have a positive body image, you probably like the way you look and accept yourself the way you are. This is a healthy attitude that allows you to explore other aspects of growing up, such as increasing independence from your parents, enhanced intellectual and physical abilities, and an interest in dating.

When you believe in yourself, you're much less likely to let your own mistakes get you down. You are better able to recognise your errors, learn your lessons, and move on. The same goes for the way you treat others. Teens who feel good about themselves and have good self-esteem are less likely to use putdowns to hurt themselves or anyone else.

A positive, optimistic attitude can help you develop better self-esteem. For example, saying, 'Hey, I'm human,' instead of 'Wow, I'm such a loser,' when you've made a mistake. Or avoiding blaming others when things don't go as expected.

Knowing what makes you happy and how to meet your goals can make you feel capable, strong, and in control of your life. A positive attitude and a healthy lifestyle are a great combination for developing good self-esteem.

Tips for boosting your self-esteem

Some teens think they need to change how they look or act to feel good about themselves. But if you can train yourself to reprogramme the way you look at your body, you can defend yourself from negative comments – both those that come from others and those that come from you. Remember: when others criticise your body, it's usually because they are insecure about the changes happening to themselves.

The first thing to do is recognise that your body is your own, no matter what shape, size, or colour it comes in. If you are very worried about your weight or size, you can check with your doctor to verify that things are OK. But remember that it is no one's business but your own what your body is like – ultimately, you have to be happy with yourself.

When you believe in yourself, you're much less likely to let your own mistakes get you down. You are better able to recognise your errors, learn your lessons, and move on

------

Remember, too, that there are things about yourself you can't change – such as your height and shoe size – and you should accept and love these things about yourself. But if there are things about yourself that you do want to change, make goals for yourself. For example, if you want to lose weight, commit yourself to exercising three to four times a week and eating nutritiously. Accomplishing the goals you set for yourself can help to improve your self-esteem.

When you hear negative comments coming from within, tell yourself to stop. Your inner critic can be retrained. Try exercises like giving yourself three compliments every day. While you're at it, every evening list three things in your day that really gave you pleasure. It can be anything from the way the sun felt on your face, the sound of your favourite band, or the way someone laughed at your jokes. By focusing on the good things you do and the positive aspects of your life, you can change how you feel about yourself.

Where can I go if I need help?

Sometimes low self-esteem and body image problems are too much to handle alone. Some teens may become depressed, and lose interest in activities or friends. Talk to a parent, coach, religious leader, guidance counsellor, therapist, or an adult friend. An adult can help you put your body image in perspective and give you positive feedback about your body, your skills, and your abilities.

If you can't turn to anyone you know, call a teen crisis hotline (check the yellow pages under social services). The most important thing is to get help if you feel like your body image and low self-esteem are affecting your life.

■ This information was provided by KidsHealth, one of the largest resources online for medically reviewed health information written for parents, kids, and teens. For more articles like this one, visit www.KidsHealth.org or else www.TeensHealth.org

© KidsHealth.org

Confidence and confidence building

People often think that if you are not confident from birth then you will never be confident at all. They could never be more wrong

A lot of people become very self-confident when something successful has happened in their lives. This is because they know that they are capable of doing something successful and they feel that they could do it again. They also feel that they are able to reach their full potential and they feel that they want to show this to other people.

If you feel that you totally lack any form of self-confidence then it would be a good idea to read the following tips:

- Set some small targets or goals for yourself. Once you have met these targets or goals you should feel more positive about yourself and then you should be able to set new targets or goals. After many small targets you should be able to set slightly bigger goals. This should help you to feel that you can do anything you want if you set your mind to it.
- Try and do new things, things that you have never done before. They don't have to be big. It could be anything from answering a question in your maths lesson (where you have never talked to the teacher before and you just sit in the corner, quite as a mouse) or it could be something drastic like jumping off a bridge (with a cord of course!). If it does succeed or not, the thought of trying something new should make you feel that you are confident enough to try new things out.
- Prepare yourself for tasks, which may need any form of confidence such as job interviews or giving talks to people of your own age. If you are fully prepared then you will come across as more relaxed to the people you are with, which automatically makes you more confident.
- A good preparation method is through role-plays. For example

---

You must remember that no one is totally confident. A lot of people manage to look confident on the outside and feel completely useless inside

---

if you were going to give a speech to your form group about how wonderful Pupiline is then write it and read it to your dog, whether he's interested or not. You could also do something similar for job interviews, ask a member of your family or a friend to pretend to be an employer who is interviewing you. This will help you to be prepared as well as helping build the confidence you need.

- Constantly remind yourself of good skills and qualities.

You must remember that no one is totally confident. A lot of people manage to look confident on the outside and feel completely useless inside. Confidence is a good skill to have and looks good on your CV but it is one quality that can always be improved. You must remember this one bit of advice, which I find myself constantly telling myself or my mates . . . 'You can do anything if you put your mind to it!'

- The above information is from Pupiline's web site which can be found at www.pupiline.net

© 1999-2003 Pupiline Limited

GREAT PRESENTATION! YOU'VE CLEARLY DONE THIS SORT OF THING BEFORE!

... WELL, IN FRONT OF THE DOG...

Self-esteem
self-evaluation survey

Information from the National Association for Self-Esteem

Please respond to the following questions using a 1-10 scale:

Lowest 1   2   3   4   5   6   7   8   9   10   *Highest*

1. Did you grow up in a family where there was much love and nurturing?
(If you did grow up in a family where there was much love and nurturing, give yourself a 9 or 10; if not, give yourself a lower score.)
1   2   3   4   5   6   7   8   9   10

2. Are you always honest with your feelings when dealing with other people?
(If you are always honest with your feelings when dealing with other people, give yourself a 9 or 10; if not, give yourself a lower score.)
1   2   3   4   5   6   7   8   9   10

3. Are you making an attempt to resolve issues in your life, issues that are of great importance to you, or are you avoiding dealing with them?
(If you are making an attempt to resolve important issues in your life, give yourself a 9 or 10; if not, give yourself a lower score.)
1   2   3   4   5   6   7   8   9   10

4. Do you ever volunteer to help others, people more needy than yourself?
(If you do help others more needy than yourself, give yourself a 9 or 10; if not give, yourself a lower score.)
1   2   3   4   5   6   7   8   9   10

5. Do you anger easily and is your anger often misdirected?
(If you do not anger easily, give yourself a 9 or 10; if not, then give yourself a lower score.)
1   2   3   4   5   6   7   8   9   10

6. How is your eye contact when interacting with others?
(If your eye contact is good, give yourself a 9 or 10; if not, give yourself a lower score.)
1   2   3   4   5   6   7   8   9   10

7. Are you a heavy smoker, or do you abuse alcohol or drugs?
(If you do not smoke or abuse alcohol or drugs, give yourself a 10, 9, or 8.)
1   2   3   4   5   6   7   8   9   10

8. Are you a risk-taker, and one who does not fear failure?
(If you are not a risk-taker and one who does fear failure, give yourself a 1, 2, or 3; if you do take risks, and do not fear failure, give yourself a higher score.)
1   2   3   4   5   6   7   8   9   10

9. Are you often ill with colds, the flu, or other minor illnesses?
(If yes, give yourself a 1, 2, or 3.)
1   2   3   4   5   6   7   8   9   10

10. When someone does something that makes you angry, do you tell them how you feel – or do you keep your feelings inside yourself?
(If you do not keep your feelings inside yourself, then give yourself a 9 or 10; if you do withhold your feelings, then give yourself a lower score.)
1   2   3   4   5   6   7   8   9   10

11. Do you speak your mind when an issue comes up about which you have strong feelings?
(If you do speak your mind, then give yourself a 9 or 10; if not, then give yourself a lower score.)
    1   2   3   4   5   6   7   8   9   10

12. Do you often find yourself telling a lie or a half-truth?
(If you do not tell lies or half-truths, then give yourself a 9 or 10; if you do, then give yourself a lower score.)
    1   2   3   4   5   6   7   8   9   10

13. Are you compassionate of other people's plights in life?
(If you are compassionate of other people's plights in life, then give yourself a 9 or 10; if not, then give yourself a lower score.)
    1   2   3   4   5   6   7   8   9   10

14. Do you ever see yourself as a victim, or do you often feel victimised by other people's actions?
(If yes, give yourself a 1, 2, or 3.)
    1   2   3   4   5   6   7   8   9   10

Calculate your score!

My score is: _____

Total Points

120-140   You more than likely have very high self-esteem.

90-120   Your self-esteem is not bad, but could definitely use some work.

Below 90   You need to look at how you're interacting with other people in your life and begin a programme
                 to build your own self-image.

*'The higher your feelings of self-worth, and the more your life is in harmony,
the closer you will perform to your skill level on a consistent basis. And it is only then
that visualisation techniques become effective.'*

Special note:
'Wagging the tail of the dog' as it applies to the misconception regarding the use of positive affirmations:
Reciting positive affirmations about yourself (and hoping for results) is like wagging the tail of a dog in hope
that tail-wagging will make the dog happy. It won't. The dog must be happy first, and then its tail will wag.

■ The above information is from the National Association for Self-Esteem's web site which can be found at
www.self-esteem-nase.org

© Marvin Fremerman, National Association for Self-Esteem (NASE)

How to give your child the gift of self-esteem

Helping your child grow up with strong self-esteem is the most important task of parenthood. As a parent, you are the primary influence on how your child feels about herself – her self-esteem.

You are a mirror of who she is. And you want your child to feel valuable, to have strong self-esteem. Kids with high self-esteem have an easier time in life. Providing a positive reflection doesn't mean you allow your child to run the family or approve of everything he/she does. It does mean that you build positive self-esteem.

Listening to your child builds self-esteem

Choose a time when you can give your child your full attention with a minimum of distractions. Invite your child to talk by asking some open-ended questions that can't be answered by 'yes' or 'no'. Then follow his lead. When you cannot take the time to listen to your child, she feels unimportant, boring, not good enough. Low self-esteem follows.

Active listening builds self-esteem

Look at your child, ask questions, and paraphrase statements. Remember to look with your eyes. Pay attention to feelings, posture, and your tone of voice.

If necessary, help a young child find words to describe his/her feelings. Don't distract yourself with details. Just listen for the point of the story and give feedback to the point.

Don't try to fix things

Children usually want to share an experience, not hear a solution. Learning to solve their own problems builds self-esteem, too.

Accepting your child builds self-esteem

When you accept all of your child, the good and the bad, your child can accept him/herself. This is the foundation of self-esteem. Train yourself to:

1. Recognise his/her unique abilities and talents.
2. Reinforce, nurture, and help the child see these talents.
3. See negative behaviour in the context of who your child is.

Focus only on changing behaviour that is important to change, i.e. behaviour that isolates or harms him/her or disrupts the family. You don't need and should not want to change everything about your child to fit your 'specs'. Again, your job is to make your child feel valuable and build self-esteem.

Use the language of self-esteem

Describe the behaviour without judging the child so that you distinguish between the child's worth and his/her behaviour. Describing behaviour gives him/her accurate feedback about actions and how actions affect the child and others. By not labelling a child as good or bad, you separate appraisals of behaviour from basic value or worth.

Share the reasons behind your reactions

It is easier for children to meet expectations and/or avoid conflict when they understand why you react they way you do. Validate your child's experience so that he/she feels seen and understood as a worthy person even when behaviour is being corrected.

Praise without overpraising to build self-esteem

Praise is what gives children the message that they are accepted and appreciated. They learn to praise themselves and recognise and value their own efforts and talents. On the other hand, overpraise creates pressure to be the 'smartest, best, most wonderful kid ever', a set-up for eventual failure. Avoid backhanded praise. This mixes praise and insult. Say, 'I'm glad you got it done,' instead of, 'It's about time.' Try, 'You look good in blue,' instead of, 'I'm glad you are wearing something besides all that black you and your friends like.'

Discipline and set limits to build self-esteem

Children who are not disciplined cannot grow up with high self-esteem. They tend to feel more dependent and also feel that they have less control over their world. Children will run into disapproval and cruelties in the world. They need the physical and emotional protection of rules and limits to grow self-esteem.

When you give your child acceptance and he/she can see you really see, value, and appreciate him/her, you have provided armour against drugs, unhealthy relationships, and delinquency.

■ The above information is from Positively MAD's web site: www.positivelymad.co.uk

© Positively MAD 2003

Can you overpraise your child?

Children have to cope with failure, says Anne Karpf

In the lexicon of childraising, one word is now taboo: failure. Parents and carers must try to prevent children from experiencing even a whiff of it. A whole newspeak has emerged to efface or disguise it. Failure is regarded like one of George Orwell's thought crimes – a crime against optimism. More and more children are raised the 'can do' way, as if they can achieve anything. But what happens when they can't?

There are childcare manuals that maintain that 'a child's self-esteem is harmed by failure'. In fact, Nicholas Emler's recent report on *Self-esteem: the costs and causes of low self-worth* (Joseph Rowntree Foundation) disproves this, finding that people's low or high self-esteem persists irrespective of their actual achievements.

But you can see why positive thinking is so beguiling. It seems to offer the prospect – no, mirage – of perpetual success. Our children can pass through life without ever falling short. This must rank, along with a self-emptying dishwasher and a volume control button on adolescents, as number one among most parents' fantasies. But there are times

when kids don't measure up and parents can't kiss it better. So, instead of trying to gird our children for a permanent sense of well-being, how do we help them deal effectively with failure?

In reality, parents deploy a gamut of strategies. Jackie Henderson, mother of three, says: 'If one of them comes back upset at some failure, I say, "You'll just have to try harder next time." I'm quite unsympathetic – it's not, "Oh darling, let's talk about this." I'm not a believer in compensation, either – here's a sweet or a present to make up for it. I'm quite brusque, but the idea is that it's not the end of the

> *Some parents are particularly skilled at shepherding their kids towards areas where they're less likely to experience failure, and helping build their confidence by 'setting up' success*

world; life's like that. We don't give prizes for disappointment.'

Margot Waddell, consultant child and adolescent psychotherapist at the Tavistock Clinic and author of *Inside Lives* (Karnac Books), recognises this approach. 'I myself as a parent would often say, "Don't worry, it doesn't matter, there are lots more important things than that", while often feeling it does matter. A child can pick up on that, so reassurance rarely works.'

Dilys Daws, honorary consultant child psychotherapist at the Tavistock Clinic, shares Henderson's reluctance to give presents to make children feel better. She says: 'Sometimes, parents have to be able to show children what it is they could do next, to move on.'

Some parents are particularly skilled at shepherding their kids towards areas where they're less likely to experience failure, and helping build their confidence by 'setting up' success. Jo Russell-Graham was so concerned that her son would label himself a failure when he didn't get into the secondary school where all his mates were headed, that she spent hours trying to help him see that

he'd struggle in a school which didn't suit him. (In the event, within one term at his new school, he'd won football colours and felt great.) Efforts like this are often undermined by a competitive, league-tables culture that ranks children like Crufts' dogs. But they might as well get used to it: competition is a fact of life that can't be dodged.

'You also don't want people to say, "You don't have to try and achieve, just be yourself, darling,"' says Daws, 'because no one would ever struggle to shine. Babies strive to do things, to achieve. The real roots of self-esteem are the parents being around and noticing it.'

The problem is that praising effort rather than achievement has become the new mantra. A 1998 study in the *Journal of Personality and Social Psychology* found that children lauded for intelligence were less prepared to deal with failure, perhaps because they saw it as proof that they weren't so intelligent after all. Those praised for their effort and hard work, on the other hand, were more likely to blame their failure on a lack of effort, and to find ways of doing better next time.

Perhaps the single most important factor shaping how our kids cope with their failures is how we deal with ours

In the event, many parents try to assuage the pain of their children's disappointments by encouraging them to learn from failure and see how to avoid it by doing things differently. While this may be a useful strategy, is it not ultimately just another way of trying to feel good about feeling bad? The fact is that some disappointments in life are damned awful and can't be brushed off or made uplifting.

But perhaps the single most important factor shaping how our kids cope with their failures is how we deal with ours. If being disappointed leads us inexorably to the

drinks cabinet, we can't expect our cherubs blithely to accommodate their own disappointments.

'A child's successes and failures often stir up anxiety in their parents,' says Waddell. 'Some parents feel so narcissistically involved and identified with their children's sense of success and failure that their own disappointment gets projected onto the child. Children are often needed by parents to live out something they haven't been able to achieve themselves. Understanding one's own disappointments and where they come from is always crucial in dealing appropriately with one's child's.'

As Russell-Graham admits: 'I felt Laurence's failure to get into that school more, in some ways, than him. I thought, "That's my stuff."'

Jennifer Silverstone, a psychotherapist, thinks it essential that we help children see that some failure is inevitable but not catastrophic. 'Parents are obliged to assist with the disillusion of the omnipotent fantasy that you can have everything and do everything if only you work hard and try to be a good person,' she says. 'You don't want to take the path of

Children are often needed by parents to live out something they haven't been able to achieve themselves

saying that it doesn't matter if you don't win or if you fail, because these things certainly do and should matter to the child. On the other hand, you don't want the child to feel that the world will come to an end if they don't get what they wanted.

'Acknowledgement is different: the idea is "I suffered, mother knows I suffered" – there's a moment of mutuality. "I'm disappointed that mother hasn't made a world where I get everything I want, but we've both survived, and I've learnt and grown that bit through it."'

Inspired, I ask if this is how she was with her kids. 'Don't be stupid!'

Ah, that moment of mutuality.

■ This article first appeared in the *Guardian*, 13 February 2002.
© Anne Karpf

Confident children blamed for social ills

By Nicole Martin

The widely held belief that low self-esteem drives children to commit violent crime and take drugs is a myth, says a report published this week. In a blow to psychologists, who for decades have blamed low self-esteem for a range of social ills, it says confident children pose a greater risk to the public and should be offered treatment.

They are more likely to be racist, fail at school, bully others and engage in drink driving and speeding, according to the report from the Joseph Rowntree Foundation.

In contrast, children with low self-esteem tended to live more solitary lives. They suffered from depression and suicidal thoughts, and struggled to form relationships. They were also more likely to be victimised.

Prof Nicholas Emler, a social psychologist at the London School of Economics, who compiled the report, said the findings showed that high self-esteem was not the 'social vaccine' that some had believed it to be.

But child protection experts disagreed with the findings, saying that self-esteem was the motivating force behind some forms of delinquency.

Michele Elliott, founder and director of the charity Kidscape, said: 'Our research has shown that few chronic bullies have high self-esteem. The vast majority of them are lashing out because of something which has happened to them. Most are very unhappy and cannot make friends.'

© *Telegraph Group Limited, London 2003*

A sense of value

Information from Care for the Family

What's the chance of your kid underachieving, dropping out of school, creating a baby when they shouldn't, acting up, turning to drugs or running with the crowd? The answer to that conversation-stopping question is: 'It all depends'.

Or to put it more positively, what's the likelihood of them building secure relationships with their peers, fulfilling their potential, staying on the rails, confidently facing new challenges and coping effectively with the frustrations and difficulties of life? The answer, again is: 'It all depends'.

Key to the future

So what does it depend on? On how they feel about themselves – positively or negatively. It's what the jargon-generators call 'self-esteem'. This is the most important quality a child can take with them into their teenage and young adult years – to feel good and confident about who they are. This one overwhelmingly crucial factor is the greatest key to their future.

The encouraging news is that your child's self-esteem is not dependent on whether they have their own bedroom, visit Disney, or own a mountain bike. But nor is it locked in their genes – with an outcome as predictable as their ability to sing in tune. The daunting news for every parent is that, for the most part, a child's view of themselves comes directly from you.

Self-esteem – or the lack of it – springs from a child's deeply ingrained experiences of how others, particularly their parents, relate to them. The words they hear and the attitudes they experience create your child's sense of their intrinsic value. The messages they pick up from you are bound to affect the way they see themselves – either positively or negatively. So how do you build up your child's sense of self-esteem?

Let them know you love them

Make sure you child knows you love them. It's never too soon to start or too late to continue. From the cradle onwards I wanted my kids to think they were the absolute 'bee's knees' so far as their dad was concerned. Today, I still want my hulking grown-up offspring to be equally sure that I love them and respect them.

And don't be fooled into thinking this slushy stuff is just for girls. Those who know about these things tell us boys need this kind of affirmation as much, if not more than girls.

Do it with words

It's not British to say how you feel. You can tell how true this is from the conversation between a husband and wife where she said, 'Darling, you never tell me you love me any more'. To which came the reply, 'I said I loved you on our wedding day. If anything changes I'll let you know!'

The penny first dropped for my wife, Rosemary, when she watched an American friend sweep up her two-year-old in her arms, and smother him with kisses while saying, 'Ian, I love you, I love you, I love you'. It was utterly not what British people do. But for Rosemary – and eventually for me – it made a huge impression.

The child knew. It was not a matter of him guessing, assuming or hoping. He knew. And he would walk taller and more confidently as a result. British or not, we followed suit.

'I'm so proud of you'

When it comes to building self-esteem, there is no substitute for simply saying as often as you can, 'I love you', 'You're great', 'I'm so proud of you'. And the best time for doing it is when your words are not a reward for anything specific they have done.

There are ways to do it with words that are not spoken and these carry even more weight. Okay, so it's not cool or British. But so what? Try a note slipped into a lunch box or into a packed bag when they are going away, or a few well-chosen lines on a birthday or Christmas card.

Don't leave it until they are in their teens. Otherwise the only response will be, 'Give it a rest, Dad! Leave it out!' The older they get, the less public they will wish you to be. But do it.

■ Based on the book *The ParenTalk Guide to being a Dad*, written by Peter Meadows.

■ This article first appeared in the *Care for the Family* magazine – Summer 2001. Visit their web site at www.care-for-the-family.org.uk

© Reproduced by permission of Hodder and Stoughton Limited

■ Relatively low self-esteem is not a risk factor for delinquency, violence towards others (including child and partner abuse), drug use, alcohol abuse, educational under-attainment or racism. (p. 6)

■ The strongest influences upon self-esteem are the individual's parents. Parenting style, physical and particularly sexual abuse play a significant role, as do genetic factors. (p. 6)

■ Self-esteem is a person's unconditional appreciation of her/himself. It matters because people who do not value themselves feel unworthy. They can then treat themselves and others badly, usually unintentionally. (p. 10)

■ People with a strong sense of self-worth and self-confidence have high levels of self-esteem, which keeps them mentally healthy and able to cope. (p. 12)

■ Healthy high self-esteem is characterised by an open mind and flexible, warm, friendly, outgoing personality with a high standard of personal conduct. There is self-respect and self-love, combined with respect for others ('You're OK, I'm OK'). (p. 14)

■ Low self-esteem is characterised by more closed, rigid and defensive (territorial hostility) behaviours and opinions. The world is repeatedly experienced as threatening, demanding or unsupportive, which leads to free-flowing anxiety or constant frustration and anger. (p. 14)

■ American research has revealed that people who consider themselves to be highly optimistic live, on average, 7.5 years longer than pessimists. (p. 15)

■ Things that give life meaning and purpose increase your chances of being happy today. (p. 15)

■ 'The relationship you have with yourself will determine the relationship you have with happiness.' (p. 16)

■ Self-esteem is an opinion not a fact. The way we view and feel about ourselves has a profound effect on how we live our lives. These opinions are shaped by experiences in the family, at school, from friendships and in wider society. Self-esteem involves our ability to think, to deal with life and to be happy. (p. 18)

■ Individuals with defensive or low self-esteem typically focus on trying to prove themselves or impress others. They tend to use others for their own gain. (p. 20)

■ Self-esteem is the feeling we have about our worth and value as a person. Self-confidence is the feeling we have about our ability to do things. In other words esteem is about your 'being' and confidence is about what we 'do'. (p. 22)

■ During adolescence many experience a significant decline in self-esteem. Studies have indicated that 85% can identify ways they would like to improve. The level of self-esteem of girls drops to as low as 29% by age 17 and to 45% for boys. (p. 25)

■ The best way to sustain a self-esteem is not to seek the approval of others but to acquire and demonstrate competence by gaining new skills and making progress towards one's goals. (p. 26)

■ Everyone experiences problems with self-esteem at certain times in their lives – especially teens who are still figuring out who they are and where they fit into the world. (p. 27)

■ Self-esteem is the greatest gift we can develop in our children because with high self-esteem anything is and will be possible. We are what we think we can be. (p. 30)

■ Some teens struggle with their self-esteem when they begin puberty. That's because the body undergoes many changes when puberty starts. These rapid changes and the desire for acceptance make it difficult for teens to judge whether they are 'normal' when they look at other teens around them. (p. 31)

■ Media images from TV, movies, and advertising may affect self-esteem. Girls may struggle with media images of teen girls and women who are unrealistically thin. Many women and teen girls in magazines, the news, or on TV are unusually thin, which may lead girls who are not thin to believe that something is wrong with them. (p. 32)

■ No one is totally confident. A lot of people manage to look confident on the outside and feel completely useless inside. (p. 33)

■ Some parents are particularly skilled at shepherding their kids towards areas where they're less likely to experience failure, and helping build their confidence by 'setting up' success. (p. 37)

ADDITIONAL RESOURCES

You might like to contact the following organisations for further information. Due to the increasing cost of postage, many organisations cannot respond to enquiries unless they receive a stamped, addressed envelope.

Care for the Family
PO Box 488
Cardiff, CF15 7YY
Tel: 029 2081 0800
Fax: 029 2081 4089
E-mail: mail@cff.org.uk
Web site: www.care-for-the-family.org.uk
Care for the Family is committed to strengthening family life, and helping those who are hurting because of family break-up.

Eating Disorders Association (EDA)
1st Floor, Wensum House
103 Prince of Wales Road
Norwich
Norfolk, NR1 1DW
Tel: 01603 619090
Fax: 01603 664915
E-mail: info@edauk.com
Web site: www.edauk.com
Eating Disorders Association is a national charity offering help, support and information to people whose lives are affected by eating disorders, in particular, anorexia and bulimia nervosa. It aims to campaign to improve standards of treatment and care and to raise awareness of eating disorders and related issues. Telephone helplines 01603 621 414 (helpline – open 9.00am to 6.30pm weekdays) 01603 765 050 (youthline callers 18 & under – open 4.00pm to 6.00pm weekdays)

The International Council for Self-Esteem
234 Montgomery Lane
Port Ludlow WA 98365
USA
Tel: + 1 360 437 0300
E-mail: Esteem1@AOL.com
Web site: www.self-esteem-international.org
The Council serves as a resource for anyone interested in research, training, materials, and resources related to self-esteem. Our purpose is to promote public and personal awareness of the benefits of a healthy sense of self-esteem and personal responsibility and to establish conditions within families, schools, businesses and governments that foster these qualities.

Joseph Rowntree Foundation (JRF)
The Homestead
40 Water End
York
North Yorkshire, YO30 6WP
Tel: 01904 629241
Fax: 01904 620072
E-mail: infor@jrf.org.uk
Web site: www.jrf.org.uk
The Foundation is an independent, non-political body which funds programmes of research and innovative development in the fields of housing, social care and social policy. It publishes its research findings rapidly and widely so that they can inform current debate and practice.

Mind
Granta House
15-19 Broadway, Stratford
London, E15 4BQ
Tel: 020 8519 2122
Fax: 020 8522 1725
E-mail: contact@mind.org.uk
Web site: www.mind.org.uk
Mind works for a better life for everyone with experience of mental distress. For a full publications list send a stamped addressed envelope to Mind Mail Order, 15-19 Broadway, London E15 4BQ, Tel: 020 8519 2122. Fax: 020 8522 1725. Mind produces a wide range of publications, including our award-winning 'Understanding' booklets, covering anxiety, depression, schizophrenia and other problems, and a 'How To' mental health promotion series. Mind's information unit has also produced a wide range of factsheets. Helpline 0345 660 163.

National Association for Self-Esteem (NASE)
Box 674
Normal, IL 61761
USA
Web site: www.self-esteem-nase.org
The purpose of this organisation is to fully integrate self-esteem into the fabric of society so that every individual, no matter what their age or background, experiences personal worth and happiness. NASE believes self-esteem is 'The experience of being capable of meeting life's challenges and being worthy of happiness'.

The Self-Esteem Institute
10175 SW Barbur Blvd.
Suite 300BI
Portland, OR 97219
USA
Tel: + 1 503 293 6608
Fax: + 1 503 925 8806
Web site: www.theselfesteeminstitute.com
Dedicated to the advancement of healthy self-esteem.

INDEX

abuse, and low self-esteem 6, 10, 12
academic achievement, and self-esteem 18, 20
adolescents *see* young people
aggressive behaviour
    avoiding 28
    and children's self-esteem 29
alcohol abuse, and low self-esteem 6, 20
anger management, and self-esteem 3, 5
assertive behaviour, and young people 28

babies, and self-esteem 1-2
behaviour patterns, and low self-esteem 6, 14, 20, 21, 29
belonging, and children's self-esteem 29
body image, and self-esteem 28, 31-2
Boots' Wellbeing 2000 study 15, 16
boys and young men
    and self-esteem 39
        levels of 25
        and personality 26
        and puberty 31
bullying
    body image and self-esteem 32
    and children's self-esteem 29, 38
    in the workplace 24

Cambridge University, students and self-esteem 18-19
Care for the Family magazine 39
celebrities, and self-esteem 8, 12
children
    and self-esteem 1-2
        advice for parents on 36, 39
        backhanded praise 36
        confident children and social ills 38
        developing 12-14, 29-30
        improving 27-8
        overpraising 36, 37-8
        praising appropriate behaviour 8-9, 36
        and undeserved praise 21
college students, and self-esteem 18-19
competence, and self-esteem 21
confidence
    and confidence building 33
    confident children and social ills 38
    self-confidence 22-4
        loss of in children 29
conversational skills 5
criticism
    and self-esteem 27
    and body image 32
culture, effects on body image and self-esteem 31-2

depression
    and low self-esteem 3, 10, 12, 13, 14
        in young people 25, 38
dieting, girls and self-esteem 11, 31
discipline, and children's self-esteem 36

divorce, and children's self-esteem 2, 14
domestic violence, and low self-esteem 3
drug abuse, and low self-esteem 6, 20

eating disorders, and low self-esteem 6, 10-11, 12, 13, 20, 25, 31
economic outcomes, and low self-esteem 6
egotism, and self-esteem 8
emotional intelligence, and self-confidence 22
Emotional Intelligence programmes 24
emotional (soft) skills, and self-esteem 5
empathy 5
exercise, and self-esteem 26, 28

failure, and children's self-esteem 37-8
false (pseudo) self-esteem 14, 20, 21
families
    and self-esteem 1-2, 12-13
        see also parents
fathers, and children's self-esteem 39
'Freeze-Framing', for eliminating stress in children 30

girls and young women
    and self-esteem
        eating disorders 11, 25
        levels of 25
        and personality 26
        and puberty 31

happy personalities 15-16
health benefits of optimism 15
human values, and self-esteem 21

immune system, and personality 15
insecurity, and low self-esteem 17-18

Joseph Rowntree Foundation 6, 38

KidsHealth
    on body image and self-esteem 31-2
    on improving self-esteem 27-8

La Belle Foundation, Self-Esteem website 9
listening, helping children to gain self-esteem 36
low self-esteem (LSE)
    and behaviour patterns 6, 14, 20, 21, 29
    children with 2, 38
    costs and causes of 6
    and eating disorders 6, 10-11, 12, 13, 20, 25, 31
    impact of 3
    and insecurity 17-18
    symptoms of 3
    therapy for 3, 7, 12

massage, and self-esteem 26
mental health, and self-esteem 10, 12

ACKNOWLEDGEMENTS

The publisher is grateful for permission to reproduce the following material.

While every care has been taken to trace and acknowledge copyright, the publisher tenders its apology for any accidental infringement or where copyright has proved untraceable. The publisher would be pleased to come to a suitable arrangement in any such case with the rightful owner.

Chapter One: Self-Esteem

The story on self-esteem, © KidsHealth.org, *About self-esteem*, © The Self-Esteem Institute, *Does 'self-esteem' really exist?*, © Uncommon Knowledge, *The costs and causes of low self-esteem*, © Joseph Rowntree Foundation (JRF), *Answering misconceptions about self-esteem*, © The National Association for Self-Esteem, *Self-esteem diamond explanation*, © La Belle Foundation, *Self-esteem and eating disorders*, © Eating Disorders Association (EDA), *Body image and appearance*, © The Guide Association, *Proportion of girls currently dieting*, © The Guide Association, *A valuable trait*, © Health Development Agency, *False self-esteem*, © 2002 Michael J. Meredith, *Happiness is all in the mind*, © Telegraph Group Limited, London 2003, *Insecurity and low self-esteem . . .* , © Uncommon Knowledge, *Self-esteem and college*, © University of Cambridge Counselling Service, *The true meaning of self-esteem*, © National Association for Self-Esteem (NASE), *Self-esteem or self-confidence*, © Buckholdt Associates.

Chapter Two: Building Self-Esteem

Adolescence – a time of crisis in self-esteem, © International Council for Self-Esteem, *How to . . . increase your self-esteem*, © MIND, *How can I improve my self-esteem?*, © KidsHealth.org, *Top tips to being assertive, not aggressive*, © Pupiline Limited, *How to develop self-esteem in children*, © Families, *Constant testing 'demotivates' pupils*, © Guardian Newspapers Limited 2002, *Body image and self-esteem*, © KidsHealth.org, *Confidence and confidence building*, © Pupiline Limited, *Self-esteem self-evaluation survey*, © Marvin Fremerman, National Association for Self-Esteem (NASE), *How to give your child the gift of self-esteem*, © Positively MAD 2003, *Can you overpraise your child?*, © Anne Karpf, *Confident children blamed for social ills*, © Telegraph Group Limited, London 2003, *A sense of value*, © Reproduced by permission of Hodder and Stoughton Limited.

Photographs and illustrations:

Pages 1, 6, 19, 39: Pumpkin House; pages 4, 7, 16, 17 22, 29, 33, 35, 37: Simon Kneebone; pages 12, 15, 24, 27: Bev Aisbett.

Craig Donnellan
Cambridge
May, 2003